POWER TOOLS
FOR FAMILIES AND FRIENDS

Building Positive Discipline
and Relationship Skills

By

Joel S. Leitch

ISBN: 1-4140-4566-2 (e-book)
ISBN: 1-4140-4565-4 (Paperback)

Library of Congress Control Number: 2003099156

This book is printed on acid free paper.

Printed in the United States of America
Bloomington, IN

1stBooks - rev.01/19/04

TABLE OF CONTENTS

FORWARD

After 22 years (so far) of counseling, pastoring, teaching, coaching, and mentoring literally thousands of people, I have come to realize that most people have pretty similar lists of frustrations and hopes for their children, their families, their friendships, and even themselves. The problem is that many people do not know where to go to get their questions answered. Unfortunately, many people would not consider going to someone else to get help, so their questions go unanswered, and their frustrations grow. I shudder to think of how many marriages and families have been miserable, maybe even to the point of falling apart, simply because people never got the answers they needed on how to make things better. The Bible says that people perish for the lack of knowledge, and I believe it. My hope is that lots of people will find the answers they are looking for in this book.

After having had the privilege, and awesome responsibility, of being the one many people came to for advice, I began to think it would be a good thing if someone would write a book that gave at least basic answers to the questions they were asking.

I finally decided that if the book was going to become reality, I might as well write it myself, since I was the one thinking it should be written. So, you are holding the compilation of a whole bunch of information filtered down into this format over many years, and through the tears of many people. My intent was to write something that would be thorough and challenging, and yet easy and enjoyable to read - I hope you find that to be true on all counts.

I think there is something for everyone in this book. If you find that one part of the book isn't for you, then just move on to another part until you find what you need. I hope also that this will be the kind of book you would want to give to friends and family so they can glean some benefit from it also.

Enjoy the ride!

DEDICATION

I thought long and hard about whom I would dedicate this book too. The idea of dedicating a book may seem rather frivolous to some, but I consider it to be a very important part of the whole process of writing a book. Writing this book was not just a casual effort for me. I have worked with literally thousands of children and parents whose lives seemed to be totally destroyed. I have seen family dysfunction of virtually every kind. I have sat with kids in jail cells in the middle of the night after being called to help. I have recommended children be removed from their homes when that is the last thing I ever wanted to see. I have counseled both suicidal children and suicidal parents who thought things could never get better.

I have also seen smiles come to faces that thought they would never form a smile again, when they found something that worked for them. I have seen families come back together who thought they never would. I have seen children become productive members of society after much of the same society had given up on them. I truly do believe there is hope for almost any family. It often takes swallowing some pride, though, and trying some difficult things. If I did not believe that, I would not have spent all the late nights and sore backs in front of my computer to complete this book. I truly want to touch people's lives with this information. So here is my dedication:

I dedicate this book first to all of you young people who have experienced a lot of heartache already because your life has lacked proper discipline. You may not like me very much at first when your parents get this book and start putting some of the principles to work. I want to encourage you to hang in there though. Change is rarely easy but can be incredibly rewarding. Try to help your parents make things better. Try not to fight them, or argue with them, when they are trying to make things better. There is nothing wrong with you studying this book also. Realize that your parents are just people too. They feel hurt, lonely, rejected, depressed, misunderstood, and scared at times … just like you. They will make mistakes along the way…just like you. Do your best to share your feelings and thoughts with them. Be sure to listen to what they are saying. No matter how much of a mess things may seem to be right now, they can get better if you will all work on it together. Do yourself and your family a favor and give it your best shot.

I also dedicate this book to you parents out there. You have such an incredible challenge if you are trying to raise responsible children in today's world. It seems like so much of what we see and hear nowadays is designed to make your parenting job more difficult. Don't despair. I choose to believe that you really do want to be the best parent possible. I know that you want to be able to look back one of these days and be proud of that person you brought into this world. The goal is not an easy one.

I hope this book helps you. There are a lot of ideas that may not seem very new to you, but it is still nice to be reminded of them now and again. Some ideas may seem really strange. Do not be afraid to give them a try anyway. Who knows, they just might work. Realize that very few things change quickly. It will take some consistent effort. It may not seem like anything is getting better for a long time. Things may even get worse for awhile as the family system resists the changes. Hang in there. Hopefully you will be able to be really glad you did. If not, then I plead the words I saw on the side of a garbage truck once: "Satisfaction guaranteed or double your garbage back!"

JOEL S. LEITCH, M.S.

MY LICENSES AND CERTIFICATIONS:

Nationally Certified Psychologist
National Board Certified Counselor
Iowa Licensed Mental Health Counselor
Oklahoma Licensed Professional Counselor
Certified Master Addiction Counselor
Board Certified Expert in School Crisis Response
Certified Clinical Criminal Justice Specialist
Certified Cognitive-Behavioral Therapist
Certified Cognitive-Behavioral School Counselor
Certified Rational Marriage & Family Therapist
Internationally Certified Alcohol & Drug Counselor
National Certified Alcohol and Drug Counselor
Oklahoma State Certified Alcohol and Drug Counselor
Certified Compassion Fatigue Specialist
Iowa Advanced Certified Alcohol and Drug Counselor
Board Certified Expert in Traumatic Stress
Certified Traumatologist
Diplomate, American Academy of Mental Health Practitioners
Diplomate, American Academy of Experts in Traumatic Stress
Individual, Group, Advanced, and Suicide Prevention, Intervention, and Postvention Training in Critical Incident Stress Management and Debriefing
Member, American Association of Christian Counselors
Ordained by Full Gospel Assemblies International, since 1985

INTRODUCTION

WHAT IN THE WORLD IS DISCIPLINE AND WHY WRITE A BOOK ABOUT IT?

* "My mother used to get so mad at me that she would scream uncontrollably at the top of her lungs until she would simply drop from exhaustion."

* "I just do not know what to do. I try my best to be a good parent but there are times I just lose it."

* "I did not intend to hit him so hard. I just did not seem to be able to control myself after the first couple times."

* "I do not think my dad likes me. He treats my brothers and sisters better than me. He lets them get away with things that I get punished for."

I have heard these comments, or ones like them, many times during counseling sessions. So many parents are so incredibly frustrated because they feel like they are bad parents. They feel terrible about it. Many others seem to at least subconsciously believe that they are not doing a very good job in their role as parent. They seem to be hungry for answers but do not know where to look to find them. If only their child had come with an owner's manual. They often get different and/or conflicting answers from different sources, so they do not know what to believe. I am convinced that most mothers and fathers want to be good parents. Many are just not sure what that means - or how to accomplish it.

Lots of parents are carrying a great deal of guilt around because they are blaming themselves for poor choices their children have made. They get a bad case of the "if onlys." i.e. "If only I would have been a better parent..." or "If only I would have done this, or that, differently."

Approaches to parenting seem to go to two extremes:

1) The first extreme is the tendency for parents to be very harsh and repressive. Their thinking seems to be that if the child has his every move controlled as he is growing up then when he gets out "on his own" he can be expected to continue diligently on that path. Of course that does not usually work. In fact, the child is more likely to rebel against all forms of control as soon as he breaks free from the parent

2) The other extreme is to let the child "be free." Let him make his own decisions and set his own priorities. "After all, he is an individual and should not be expected to conform to what someone else wants, or expects, of him." That child is equally likely to end up with big problems. As he develops more autonomy, and has more options available to him, he will likely lack the self-control necessary to function in a society of rules.

Going to either of those extremes will destine both you and your child to many years of unhappiness. Every possible combination of discipline responses falls between those two extremes. No wonder parenting gets so frustrating at times.

The challenge, then, becomes one of finding the approach that fits your child. You will find that each child needs to be responded to in an individual way. What works for one child may not work for another child at all.

I hope this book will help you sort through the maze that exists between those two extremes. You will find lots of ideas enclosed that may seem a little radical. You may find yourself laughing sometimes, and crying sometimes, as you relate to something that is said. Do not be afraid to try some things. Sit down and read a chapter together with your children, and then talk about how it fits you as a family. Find what works and ignore the rest.

This book is also designed to help those of you who may be working or relating with young people who are not part of your immediate family. Some of you probably do a huge amount of parenting with kids who are not your own - you may be a teacher, youth pastor, little league coach, cub scout or boy scout leader, boss, or any number of other roles that has you interacting with young people. My desire is that you find lots of ideas in this book that will help you understand and interact more effectively in any of those roles.

For the rest of you - this book is for you also! There are lots of ideas in this book that could be very beneficial in your every day interactions with people. You'll find that the communication, discipline, and other issues discussed in this book are relevant for anyone who interacts with other people on any level. The discipline issues discussed may be from the perspective of parents working with their kids, but are just as important for anyone who has a leadership role over other people of any age. Just insert your name, or your particular relationship to another person, everywhere you read the word 'parent' in this book and it should make good sense to you.

So, there is something in this book for everyone! I had a horrible time giving a title to this book because it covers such a wide variety of topics, and yet all related, for such a wide variety of people. Whatever the title...whatever role you play in life...I hope the information contained within is helpful to you.

CHAPTER ONE

THE GOAL OF DISCIPLINE

Discipline is not a dirty word when it is practiced correctly. The problem is that discipline had acquired a bad reputation because so many have abused it. The goal of discipline is to help children (or anyone else for that matter) develop a self-controlled, responsible approach to life. That does not happen easily or quickly. We all know of situations where several children, all from the same family, ended up with very different personalities and responses to life even though they were all raised basically the same. Each child will ultimately choose what type of person he will be. The parents, though, can certainly contribute a strong influence during the years when those decisions are most likely to be made. The trick, if it can be called that, is for the parents, or whoever has influence over another person, to provide a well-balanced approach to their discipline.

I never cease to be amazed at the diversity of children that can come from the same family. One child may be very pleasant, intelligent and responsible. Another child from the same family could be the poster child for the Adolescent Antisocial Club of America.

PARENTAL SELF-DISCIPLINE

Let me stick my neck out early and see how many of you would like to chop it off already. One of the biggest problems with parents being able to administer discipline with their children is that they lack discipline in their own lives. When parents are being really honest with me, they will frequently make very blatant statements to that effect. They say things like, "I know what I should be doing, but it is so hard to follow through with it." or "I do not want to have an argument, so I just give in to him." They acknowledge that somewhere along the way they began to feel like they were losing control. By that time, though, they already had a problem.

1

One of the most difficult parenting challenges is to try to change a child's attitude that is already well developed.

Maybe this would be a good place to give you a little warning. This book may include a lot of ideas that are new to you. You may even be tempted to implement some of the ideas in your family. You can expect to have a war on your hands if you try to move too quickly with any of these ideas. It will not be a matter of simply choosing a new response to old behaviors. Your children have developed entire thought processes, and behavioral patterns, in response to your parenting style. Do not expect them to be all excited when you suddenly want to make a bunch of changes. You may see how some changes may be helpful. They may only see that their world is being shaken from the inside out. Sit down with your family to discuss changes before they are implemented. Explain what you want to do, and why. Your success level will likely be much higher if you let them be part of the process. They might not like it any better, but at least they will be part of the process.

CHANGING TIMES

Discipline challenges have definitely changed over the years. Look at the table below to see how extreme those changes have been.

TOP SEVEN PROBLEMS IN PUBLIC SCHOOLS - THEN AND NOW

1940	1988
1. Talking	1. Drug Abuse
2. Chewing Gum	2. Alcohol Abuse

3. Making Noise   3. Pregnancy

4. Running in the halls   4. Suicide

5. Getting out of line   5. Rape

6. Wearing improper clothes   6. Robbery

7. Not putting paper in wastebasket 7. Assault

ONE DAY IN THE LIVES OF AMERICA'S CHILDREN

Every day in the United States:

* 2,795 teenagers get pregnant
* 1,106 teenage girls have abortions
* 372 teenage girls have miscarriages
* 689 babies born to women who have had inadequate prenatal care
* 719 babies are born at a low birth rate (less than 5# 8 oz)
* 67 babies die less than one month old
* 105 babies die before their first birthday
* 27 children die as a direct result of poverty
* 10 children are killed by guns
* 30 children are wounded by guns
* 6 children commit suicide
* 135,000 children bring a gun to school
* 7,742 teenagers become sexually active
* 623 teenagers get syphilis or gonorrhea
* 211 children are arrested for drug abuse
* 437 children are arrested for drinking or drunk driving
* 1,512 teenagers drop out of school
* 1,849 children are abused or neglected
* 3,288 children run away from home
* 1,629 children are in adult jails
* 2,556 children are born out of wedlock

    *   2,989 children see their parents divorced

Source: Children's Defense Fund (information from The Almanac of the Christian World, Tyndale House, 1991-1992 edition)

It is easy to see that the parenting challenges of today are far more severe than they were just a few years ago. Families today seem to be under an almost relentless attack from outside influences that seem to be designed to destroy family unity and discipline. Parents must be very alert to the challenges and must be equipped to respond to them in the most effective way possible.

The goal of discipline, then, is to help children grow into adult individuals that are respectful, responsible, and self-disciplined. Children will never feel good about themselves unless they learn to respect limits, and to control their own desires. The children who believe that happiness only comes from getting their own way, then, will never be satisfied. They will likely develop into frustrated, angry people because there will always be times when they do not get their way. If they grow up learning to take advantage of, or manipulate, people to get their desires met, they will likely end up unloved, unloving, and very much alone.

Now, before you think I am some kind of a mean ogre or something, let me put some balance to this. Children do need to feel happiness. Hopefully they will feel significantly more happiness than unhappiness. Discipline, however, must come first. That may sound like a contradiction, but it is not. Happiness is a by-product of discipline.

The child who is disciplined consistently and appropriately will be much more likely to experience happiness than the child without. With that perspective it is easy to see that discipline is something you do FOR a child, not just what you do TO a child.

4

CHAPTER TWO

SPECIAL DISCIPLINE ISSUES

Before we get too far into what discipline is and what it is not, I would like to spend a little time discussing some special issues that relate to discipline. Covering these now will help you better understand some of the things I will say later.

A. THE POWER OF THE TONGUE

I want to make sure we do not forget the terrible force of the tongue. From personal experience I can say that a tongue lashing often hurts far more than a physical beating. I have seen so many children absolutely destroyed by the words of an insensitive parent or teacher. I have heard children being screamed at with such statements as "You are worthless!" "You will never amount to anything." "You are stupid!" or "Why can't you be more like your brother?" To say those kinds of things to a child, who is likely to believe them, is nothing short of verbal child abuse. I don't know how true it is, but I heard something once that I have no problem believing: Someone said that if you hear something negative about yourself seven times from a person you consider to be a credible source (whether you like them or not) you will begin to believe it. But you have to hear something positive about yourself eleven times, from someone you consider to be a credible source, before you begin to believe it. So just stop to consider that for a moment. Which do you hear most - positive or negative? Which do you speak most - positive or negative? Many of you probably answer that you hear or speak much more negative than positive. Is it any wonder, then, that so many people have a very negative perspective of themselves and their lives?

Children need, and are hungry for, a feeling of being accepted by their parents and others around them. When those people lash out and say cruel, demeaning things, they are attacking on a personal level instead of dealing with behavior, and doing incredible harm. It is a very valuable discipline technique to learn to separate the child's behavior from whom he is as a person. To attack the value of the person will never be a positive discipline technique. Be very clear with the child that you disapprove of the behavior but still love and accept him. When you have attacked the very self-concept of a child, you have done damage that could take many years to heal. Many people live their entire lives carrying emotional scars they received years before as young children. The age-old statement "Sticks and stones may break my bones, but words will never harm me" is not true at all. A more accurate statement might be "Sticks and stones may break my bones, but words can break my heart."

B. PREDICTABILITY OF CONSEQUENCES

I am a big believer that a person should have a good idea of what consequences he can expect for wrong behaviors. Too many parents administer what might be called arbitrary, or "open-ended," consequences. An example of that might be the child who is sent to his room as a consequence for a wrong behavior without having any idea how long he will have to stay there. It ends up being like an open-ended prison sentence.

I worked with a large family once who did this a lot. A marriage brought two parents of four children each together. The new stepmother tended to resent the father's children. I noticed that one of the small boys was spending a lot of time in his room. When I asked the mother how long he had to stay in there, she responded with "Until he learns to be good." Even I couldn't figure out what that meant exactly or how it would be decided when and/or if that criteria had been met. It soon became evident to me that there was not much that boy could do to please her. Since she really did not want to be bothered by the responsibility of parenting him, she just sent him to his room. When he got sent to his room there was no way for him to predict how long he would be in there. She would just get more upset with him when he asked to come out. That was very inappropriate and unfair parenting.

Parents who just pick arbitrary kinds, or amounts, of consequences are simply not being fair to the child and are setting themselves up for further arguments and frustration. Even the laws of the land are aware of the need for this. Signs along the highway tell us exactly what our fine will be if we go over the speed limit by predefined amounts. Thick volumes of law books tell us exactly what the minimum and maximum fines and jail times will be for virtually every illegal behavior imaginable. When those guidelines are not followed, you can be sure that some civil rights group will be making a lot of noise about it. I think it should be the same way with our children. They should know what consequences they are risking when they are thinking about doing something they should not do. Of course the ultimate goal is for the child to choose to do what is right because of his desire to be right, instead of a desire to avoid the consequences of doing wrong.

C. HELPLESSNESS

I have worked with children of dysfunctional families for many years. Those dysfunctions took the form of anything from alcohol and other drug addictions, verbal, physical, and sexual abuse, domestic violence, eating and mental disorders, and virtually every other kind of family dysfunction imaginable.

Several years ago I was a Family Support Specialist in Tulsa, Oklahoma. I spent my time trying to help youth and families who were truly at the end of their ropes. In most cases at least one of the children had been involved with the Juvenile Court system and several mental health centers and counselors before they were referred to me. Many of the kids were dangerously close to being taken out of the family because their behaviors and attitudes had become too disruptive to the rest of the family. The families ranged anywhere from total poverty level to the very financially comfortable. They lived in houses that were little more than shacks to very nice houses in beautiful neighborhoods. Frequently there were other children in the family who were seen as being socially and behaviorally well-adjusted children.

I began to notice some things that were common in every family, regardless of race, financial condition, or social level. Without fail there was frustration in the family that came from feeling helpless. This feeling of helplessness usually seemed to be experienced by both the parents and the children.

The parents often reported feeling helpless about the possibilities of being able to change anything about their child. They often described how they had tried everything they could think of but nothing had worked. They often compared their children, and pointed out how, with supposedly the same discipline techniques being utilized for all the children, some were doing fine and some were not doing well at all. One child in the family may be on the honor roll at school and excelling in sports or some other activity. Another child may be failing in school, if he is not refusing to go, that is. One child has positive friendships and relationships while the other one hangs around the kids in school or the neighborhood who have the worst reputations.

The children, on the other hand, also expressed high levels of frustration and helplessness. They would often go into long explanations of how they had tried to please their parents or teachers with little or no success. They would say things like "I get into trouble no matter what I do, so why should I keep trying?" They would often resist getting involved in the counseling process because they had been through so many other counselors before, and nothing had worked. A child would often express anger and/or jealousy at one or more of their siblings because they were getting all of the positive attention. You have probably heard before that some children learn that the only way they can get attention is by doing something wrong. How sad that some kids have learned that negative attention is preferable to no attention at all.

8

Many of the kids were surprisingly candid at admitting that they had learned to take advantage of their parents' feelings of frustration and helplessness. They had learned to capitalize on those emotions to get their own way. Kids know when the parent has surrendered to the feelings of helplessness. At that point the child knows that he can simply do as he wishes, because the parent has given up on trying to maintain any control anyway.

D. EMPOWERMENT

Family situations will only get worse if parents surrender their parental rights and responsibilities to their children. If we are to ever expect things to change positively for families, it will be very important for parents to regain their rightful positions and responsibilities as the parent. Parents have a rightful and legal position of authority over their children. Just knowing that does not make anything better though. If the parents have surrendered their authority over their children then it becomes critical to begin a process to regain that authority. I have no fantasies about that being an easy process.

Feelings of frustration and helplessness may be good indicators that parents have surrendered at least some of their authority. They have probably relegated that authority to someone else, usually their children. It becomes a question of who is truly in control. Is the dog wagging the tail or is the tail wagging the dog?

When a parent surrenders his authority to the child, he can expect things to rapidly disintegrate. He can be sure that trouble awaits in the very near future.

I hear many teachers express some of these same feelings of frustration and helplessness. Discipline styles have been so drastically changed through legal process that teachers find it much more difficult to maintain their position of authority with the children in their classrooms. Things are fine when the child conforms to the

9

expectations in the school. Those same things can deteriorate very quickly, though, if there is a child who has learned to rebel against authority and is used to controlling things himself.

I have talked with many teachers whom, with tears in their eyes, expressed their dismay about feeling they have very little, if any, recourse in the area of discipline. The best they can do in most cases is to send the child to the principal's office. The principal can then, at best, talk to the child about his behavior and encourage him to change the behavior. The principal can threaten to expel the child from school, but that rarely has the desired effect either.

E. HAPPINESS

So let's talk more about what may be happening with these children and their families. Why do so many parents feel out of control when it comes to responding to the behavior and attitudes of their children?

Many parents seem to have a mistaken idea of what it means to be a good parent. Frankly, a high percentage of parents seem to feel like they are terrible failures as parents. Much of that feeling may simply come from how they define what it means to be a successful parent. Many parents discuss their feelings of failure in terms of the happiness of their children. If their kids are not happy all the time, then that is viewed as a failure on the parent's part. Consequently, the parent becomes so motivated to keep the child happy that he compromises the other parenting needs of the child.

If you are always trying to keep your child happy, you are very likely to avoid dealing with the negatives appropriately. It becomes easier to just ignore the negatives rather than risk having the child get upset or angry with you when you try to discipline him. Consequently, the child quickly learns that he can get away with many things and will ultimately end up just running roughshod over you and your discipline efforts. You will likely end up feeling trapped, and likely therefore, helpless. It is not always possible to keep your child happy and discipline him at the same time. Many a parent has been reduced to tears trying. I would suggest that it is much more useful to have your child respect you than to always like you.

When discussing possible parenting responses with a frustrated parent, I often hear statements like, "Well, I tried that before and it did not work." Underlying that statement seems to be the fear that "nothing I do will work." I have even heard parents say that they had resigned themselves to the fact that they had lost that child. Now they were just trying to wait until the child was old enough to leave home. How sad that so many people are living their daily lives with those kinds of feelings and thoughts. Is it any wonder that so many families end up falling apart under these conditions?

I remember one case that is a good example of what I am talking about. I was called in to respond to a family situation involving a 15 year old boy. He had been through several adolescent treatment centers, had tried suicide several times, and finally failed regular school because he refused to go most of the time. From there he was enrolled in an alternative school for 'troubled' kids. He finally was expelled from that school because of violent behavior toward both teachers and other students. When I arrived at the house, the kid was reclining on the couch, obviously trying to impress me with his lack of concern. When he spoke, it was with a very rebellious attitude and tone of voice. I got the feeling he was challenging me to change him as he lit a cigarette and used very socially inappropriate language. His mother and step-dad were also in the room. They would occasionally say things to the boy like "I told you not to talk that way," or "Now you know you should not think that way." Surprisingly, the boy did participate a little in the conversation. He said the reason that he did not go to school was that his mother would not buy him a motorcycle. He was unimpressed when I suggested that he may need to prove a higher level of responsibility before a motorcycle could be considered. He had a ready answer. He said he had proved he had a high level of responsibility the night before when he had helped his mother move some boxes.

11

To try to reason with this boy would be futile. It was fully ingrained in his thinking that he was in control, and things ought to go the way he wanted them to go. His parents expressed realistic feelings of frustration and total helplessness. Further discussion revealed that the parents were afraid to upset their child. They said over and over again how much they wanted him to be happy. He was not happy during their prior attempts to discipline so they stopped. They cried as they said they just did not know what they could do to "make him happy anymore." Their desire for him to be happy had totally undermined their attempts to parent him.

Later in this book we will discuss very specific ways to approach some of these challenges. This book, by design, will be talking a lot about parenting styles and techniques. My goal is not to attack parents. I know that most parents are doing the very best they know how. My goal is not to label someone a good parent or a bad parent. My goal is simply to identify some things parents can try in their families or what parents may need to discontinue doing. Hopefully I can help you see where alternative responses to certain behaviors and attitudes may yield more positive results.

F. PARENTAL GUILT TRIPS

I have already stated that many parents feel like they have failed as a parent. As a result of those feelings of failure, they feel guilty, and can get on what I will call a "guilt trip." Kids are generally very quick to identify when a parent is on a guilt trip about his parenting. They are equally quick to take advantage of that guilt trip to manipulate the parent.

Parents may begin to allow certain inappropriate behaviors to go unchallenged because of their feelings of guilt. At that point they are opening themselves up to many more problems. Most of those parents will have all sorts of justifications for letting their children get away with things that should be confronted.

Statements like "they need their freedom," or "they are just going through a phase," can be an indication that behavior that should be confronted is instead being explained away as being "part of life." Understanding that the definition of appropriate or inappropriate may change from one setting to the next, I still maintain that there is never an appropriate time for inappropriate behaviors. Instead of reinforcing the idea that there is right and wrong behavior, regardless of age or maturity level, the child learns that there are acceptable excuses for inappropriate behavior.

CHAPTER THREE

BALANCED DISCIPLINE

There is a bit of a dilemma that arises when we talk about balanced discipline. I will call it the Dilemma of Discipline. Harsh or unloving discipline can wound a child's spirit and we certainly do not want that to happen. Reluctance to exercise parental authority, however, can be equally detrimental. Either extreme can lead to heartache for both the parent and the child. Either extreme will likely lead to rebellion from the child. The dilemma, therefore, is to learn to balance discipline techniques in a way that do not go to either extreme, but still maintain a consistency somewhere between those two extremes.

BALANCED DISCIPLINE - WHAT IT IS AND WHAT IT IS NOT

So what is, and what is not, balanced discipline? To best answer that question, we had better review again the goal of discipline:

We discipline children in order to help them choose desirable behaviors in the home and in society. We discipline them in order to help them develop the internal desire to avoid unacceptable behaviors and attitudes.

The goal of discipline with children is to encourage their growth as respectable, responsible, self-disciplined individuals. We do not discipline just to get them to do what we want them to do. Part of the goal is to help them develop a personal desire to make good decisions. Many times along the course of their lives, their personal decisions will impact every other part of their life. Their ability to make quality choices for themselves will largely determine who they are as people. They quickly learn that the decisions they make in school and at home determine the quality of their interactions with their environment. The idea is to try to guide and direct them in a direction where they develop the desire and skill to make quality decisions.

14

Let me define what I mean by a "quality decision":

> A "quality decision" is a decision that is made only after considering each possible option relating to the issue at hand. As each option is considered, the possible consequences are taken into account. The impact each option would have on other people is also of paramount importance as it is considered. When a quality decision has been made, the person making it is fully prepared to accept, and live with, the outcome.

The better a person gets at making quality decisions, the less he has to spend time suffering the consequences of poor decisions.

Children cannot develop healthy self-esteems if they do not learn to respect limits and to control their own desires. The child who gets everything he wants, when he wants it, will likely end up a very unhappy person. If he is allowed to assume that happiness and satisfaction comes only from getting his own way, he will likely grow up frustrated and bitter. There will be plenty of times when he does not get his own way.

The closer children get to an age where they start making decisions that directly affect their lives, the more they must realize that they really do not have the freedom to do just whatever they want all the time. If we give kids the idea that they really do have that freedom, that they can do just about anything they want to do, then it will be a great shock to them when reality rears its ugly head. They will get angry and bitter first. Then they will likely look for someone else to blame for their predicament. The natural next step is to rebel against these limits on their behavior. The person or situation trying to establish the controls will be blamed for being unfair, uncaring, and unreasonable. That person is usually the parent or teacher who is trying to limit behaviors. By then, though, the die has been cast and is very difficult to change. A power struggle will likely ensue at that point. And so the war begins. If these kids are permitted to satisfy

15

their human potential for selfishness, they will no doubt grow up to be very lonely and unhappy individuals.

Children do need to experience a certain level of happiness. That happiness, though, needs to be achieved in the proper context of discipline. In the long run, it is discipline that makes true happiness possible.

A child needs to learn the self-discipline to:

1. Look at the situation at hand.

2. Think through the possibilities of that situation.

3. Make a positive decision based on his evaluation of the situation.

4. Act on his decisions.

5. Evaluate the outcome of his decisions so he can refine his decision to have the most positive effect on his life and on the lives of those around him.

When he learns to consider positive morality and social expectations during his decision making process, then he is a lot closer to being able to experience true happiness. Only then can he experience the self-satisfaction that comes when the desired results are achieved.

When a child enters into various life situations without having learned how to make proper decisions, he will soon find himself suffering the consequences of poor decisions. He will find that circumstances control him instead of him being able to exercise a proper level of control over them. This, of course, will lead to frustration, confusion, and bitterness. Unfortunately, he will have also quite likely already learned to blame society or circumstances for what is happening to him, rather than accepting responsibility for himself.

CHAPTER FOUR

DISCIPLINE VS PUNISHMENT

It is important at this point to talk about the difference between discipline and punishment. They are definitely NOT the same, even though many people seem to use the words interchangeably. One purpose of discipline is to encourage children to develop mature levels of responsibility in their lives.

Punishment is designed to inflict physical and/or emotional pain into a person's life as a consequence for a behavior which has been deemed "wrong" by the punisher. Punishment tends to try to obtain obedience from someone by brute force. I have to wonder how much the punisher is concerned about love or understanding while inflicting the punishment. Punishment can become more of a "bully" tactic inflicted upon someone who is unable to defend himself. It would seem to have as its slogan "Might makes right."

Punishment works while children are young and small. They will respond to what amounts to scare tactics. There is not much else you can do with a child who is still too young to understand your explanations of what is expected of him. Those children will likely be compliant with rules and expectations simply because they are afraid of the consequences. That will not work as well, though, once the child is old enough to reason with you.

We have stated before that discipline is not what a parent does *to* a child but instead it is what parents do *for* their child. It is very important to distinguish the difference between discipline and punishment. Discipline is designed to encourage children to mature responsibility.

Punishment seeks retribution for misbehavior. Punishment attempts to secure obedience by shear force, without much effort at communicating love and understanding. It is the age-old process of imposing something undesirable on a child for doing something he is not supposed to do. As the child gets older and larger, the level of force required grows as well, until force simply is not an option any more - so what do you do then? I have heard several parents say "Well, he is getting too big for me to spank anymore. It used to be that when he would mouth off to me I could give him a smack across the face but he is too big for that now." They may say that with a smile on their face, but the underlying frustration is evident. You can sense the parent's fear when they say things like "What am I going to do now? I used to be able to control him, but now he is getting bigger than I, and he is still going to be at home for another four or five years." The fear in that statement is evident. This is likely a situation where the parent has relied too much upon punishment in the past, and not enough on discipline. Now it has become a large problem for the whole family, and is likely to get even worse as time goes on. Punishment may accomplish compliance with rules for a while, but that is all. Sooner or later the child is going to rebel.

VERBAL PUNISHMENT

Remember that punishment by force can include verbal as well as physical blows. Parents who try to verbally intimidate their child into doing their desires are asking for trouble also. So many children grow up hearing their parents scream things like "You will never amount to anything." "You are worthless." "You are no good." "Can't you do anything right?", and of course the old favorite "I hope you end up having ten kids just like yourself." I guess the effort on the parent's part is to try to shame the kid into changing his behavior. What is really happening, though, is nothing short of verbal child abuse and will never lead to positive results. Verbally demeaning a child will never be a positive way to discipline.

Discipline builds relationships by correcting the behavior while accepting the person. As you consider this process, it is very important that you separate the person from the behavior. The response to the person should be very consistent even though the responses to the behaviors may vary with each of his different behaviors. It is very important to be consistent with this process so the child gets a very clear message that he is accepted and loved even though, his behavior may not be.

When you are communicating to the child that his behavior is not acceptable, be careful not to give him the message that he is a failure as a person. Punishment risks rejecting the child who has behaved undesirably, which results in alienation. Discipline focuses on present learning opportunities without harshness. Punishment focuses on the person, causing emotional hurt. Discipline displays anger appropriately against the deed and not the doer. Punishment displays anger against the doer and uses power to justify the end.

IS IT O.K. TO BE ANGRY?

Maybe I had better clarify something about anger at this point. Notice I have not said that anger is not acceptable. I have heard parents say that they feel so guilty when they get angry. Anger is a normal emotion. There are times when you may very justifiably feel helpless and angry. It is a natural response to feel at least a little helpless when you see something continue to happen that you have tried very hard to extinguish in a child's behavior or attitude patterns.

Being angry, however, does not excuse us from our responsibility to respond appropriately. It is very important to make it your first priority to handle your own emotions and behavior correctly before you try to do something about someone else's emotions and behaviors. If not, you will likely respond to the situation inappropriately and do more harm than good.

Discipline allows for cooperation and mutual respect to occur. Punishment can set up power struggles and cycles of revenge and counter-revenge. I have known children who literally sat for hours contemplating ways to get revenge on their parents. Of course that kind of relationship between parents and their children can only lead to miserable times.

Many children grow up spending their entire lives with anger seething inside, which in turn affects every other relationship they ever have. When that child finally gets away from home and feels free to do as he chooses, he is likely to engage in all sorts of socially inappropriate behavior. It is as if they are making up for lost time. They leave home almost like an explosion waiting for a place to happen.

You do not have to be some terrible, maladaptive child to have that happen. In fact, I suspect that virtually every child goes through some degree of that as they experiment with growing levels of independence. The child who has developed self-discipline, however, will be able to temper his behavior and maintain a socially acceptable behavior pattern.

THREATS

Let's discuss the concept of making threats. Many parents really damage their credibility with their children when they make threats - especially if they do not follow through with them.

Never make threats or promises that you do not keep. That is one of the fastest ways possible to teach your child to not listen to what you are saying. If he learns that you do not really mean what you are saying, then your words will fall on deaf ears. That, unfortunately, will just raise your level of frustration which, in turn, is likely to increase the severity of your threats. Of course those threats will also be ignored, and so around and around you go. That pattern will continue to escalate until there is a major explosion of some kind, and everyone will end up miserable.

Even idle threats that obviously are not meant as fact should be avoided. So many parents say things like "If you do not straighten up I am going to kill you." Even though that obviously(?) is not intended as a direct threat in most cases, it is still counter-productive. It is nothing but a feeble effort to stake a claim of ultimate power over a person, even when stated as a so-called joke.

THE SPIRIT OF THE CHILD

It is very important to be sensitive to what is happening with/to the spirit of the child. A wounded spirit is a terrible thing. A person will heal from physical hurts long before his injured spirit will heal. The injured spirit of a child takes much longer to heal than a physically injured child.

There are children who, for the rest of their lives, carry the graphic memories of something that was done, or said, to them that hurt them to the very core of their being. It may have been something that was said in haste and in anger, but still tears at the very core of the person as a human being. It may have been something said in haste that planted a seed of doubt or hurt that never stopped growing as the person grew older.

Let me summarize all of this information in a chart now so you can more easily compare what we mean when we use the words discipline and punishment.

PUNISHMENT VS DISCIPLINE CHART

PUNISHMENT	DISCIPLINE
Motivates by creating fear.	Motivates by consistent kindness and firmness.
Leads to power struggles and desire for revenge.	Permits mutual respect and cooperation to take place.
Vents anger aimed at the person instead of dealing with the	Emphasizes the need to change the behavior while remembering

21

behavior.

Focuses on disobedience in a way that can cause hurt.

Can alienate the child who has misbehaved.

the value of the person.

Focuses on the opportunity for learning from the experience.

Allows for strengthening the relationship between parent and child while correcting the wrong behavior.

CHAPTER FIVE

REWARD AND PUNISHMENT

Many parents rely on punishment as a way of handling their children's misbehavior. The same parents will usually rely on a system of reward for promoting good behavior. Read carefully now because there is a fine line to observe when discussing this. Rewarding good behavior is healthy and good. Society at its best operates on this standard and there is nothing wrong with parents doing it also.

The challenge is this: it is very important that we be careful how we reward good behavior. A lot of parents seem to try to buy good behavior from their children. They fall into the trap of buying the child more and more things in response to desired behaviors. They give them more and more money, or more and more things, as if to pay them for their appropriate behavior.

The problem develops when parents use rewards for good behavior as their primary motivator and their primary reinforcers. That can lead to some serious problems.

REWARD SYSTEM DANGERS

Let's take a look at some of the things to be careful of when using a reward system. There is a danger that it will teach the child that he should be rewarded whenever he does something good. The other side of that is that he will likely expect to have something negative occur when he does something not so good. Now this may work well when you are training rats to push levers in a cage, but it can quickly reach the extreme with humans. The danger is that all of life may start being approached as a business deal. The thinking can become "I will only do good things if there is a payoff in it for me." or "It is all right for me to do something wrong as long as the consequence is not too bad." It is easy for the child to begin to expect his parents to pay him monetarily, or in some other way, for doing things that he should be expected to do anyway.

It is a very bad practice to pay a child for cleaning his room, taking out the garbage, or doing other things to be helpful around the house. We will talk later about the concept of allowances, and I'll give some suggestions for how to tie them into the child's functioning around the house.

It is really unfair to the child to teach him that he should be paid for doing things that he should be accepting as part of his responsibilities anyway. Why should a child expect to be paid for cleaning off the table after dinner when his mother did not get paid for making the meal?

Payment may be reasonable when the child is asked to do something above and beyond the normal expectations of being a part of the family, but even then it is counter-productive to be extreme. Should we be paid for stopping at a stop sign when we are driving down the street? Of course not. It is a normal part of living in this society, and the reward is in being able to drive down that street. The consequences are swift and sure if we choose to drive down that street without accepting our responsibilities to the people around us.

It produces positive character in a child to realize and accept that he has a responsibility to the family and society he lives in. The reward is in the living. The child who grows up expecting a reward for all of his good behaviors will have a very rude awakening when he gets out on a job or other social settings. As well-adjusted people, we should know that there are many things we do simply because they are the right thing to do.

We should know and accept that there are things we should not do simply because they are not right. To not do something wrong simply because we fear being caught, and having to suffer the consequences, reveals a poor character.

We are all part of a society or culture, part of a family, part of a class at school, or part of an employment situation. As a result of being part of that group or culture, we must accept the associated responsibilities.

BRIBERY

Rewards are often administered by the parent to bribe the child instead of to solve the problem. Reward and punishment used selfishly by the parent to get their own way reinforces selfishness in the child. They are paying the child off to get him to do something they want to have done. Even children have no trouble seeing that as a very selfish behavior. The child will soon learn to use that same behavior against his parent. At times it can almost end up being extortion as the child begins to demand more and more from the parent to get the same behavior. The developing selfishness in the child may end up being a far more severe problem that the original problem.

GETTING EVEN

Children sometimes use punishment from others as a justification to continue doing inappropriate behavior. The concept is one of "getting even." Their perception is that they need to look for ways to "even the score" for being punished. This again brings up the idea of getting revenge when they do not like what someone has done to them. This is a very unhealthy thought process and can lead to very inappropriate behaviors and attitudes.

The reward and punishment process can also lead a child to the understanding that being accepted as a member of the family is solely dependent upon his performance. This, in turn, can lead to feelings of frustration, inadequacy, and rejection.

It is very unhealthy for a child to feel like he needs to do something positive in order to receive positive reinforcement from the family. The positive behavior should be a fruit of his appreciation for being part of the family, instead of being a bargaining chip for being accepted by the family.

Under those conditions, do not be surprised when he ends up with a very poor self-concept. He will likely conclude that his value as a person is based solely upon what he does rather than on whom he is.

NEGATIVE ATTENTION

I never cease to be amazed at how many children are literally starving for some attention from their family. Unfortunately, many children learn that getting negative attention is better than getting no attention at all. They find that the pain of being physically punished is less than the pain of feeling rejected or left out by parents or family. I suspect that a higher percentage of children than we would like to admit actively and deliberately seek out ways to get in trouble. They know that the consequences of negative behavior will include some "meaningful" interaction and attention from a parent. They do not want the trouble or punishment. They just want the attention. They are not so much a trouble-maker as they are a lonely child.

In this fast-paced, latch-key society children are often left to fend for themselves in virtually every way. When they spend four, five, or even six or more hours per day watching television, and an average of only a few seconds per day having quality interaction with their parents, we should not be too surprised when they are hungry for more attention from their parents. Just the fact that they are watching that much television should help us understand why children have some of the attitudes they often have.

The majority of television programming reinforces a poor value system. It will not be long before the child will be looking for some kind of reality outside of television. Television teaches the child that he should have instant gratification to all of his wishes. Television teaches that any problem can be resolved in a very short period of time and turn people into heroes in the process. When life at home does not fit into that mold there will likely be problems.

It would be easy to say, then, that they should simply watch less television, but that is not enough. It takes the efforts of the entire family to develop a positive way to meet the emotional needs of the members of that family.

The weaknesses of the reward and punishment system are easily seen in American culture today. Our materialistic and manipulative society reinforces the idea that our goal in life is to grab all the rewards you can without getting caught. Moral principles are short circuited by the effort to get by with the least pain and the most profit.

NATURAL CONSEQUENCES AND PUNISHMENT

In spite of all that has been said so far, the punishment factor is still a part of life and cannot be ignored. Based on the options we have, we make many of our decisions based upon what consequences we are willing to accept. How many people have watched their speed as they drove down the road knowing that they were speeding? They compare their speed with how much of a fine their pocketbooks can handle. The question is not whether or not they speed, but how much they can afford to break the law.

If we are motivated to change behavior because of our fear of the corresponding punishment, then we are really missing the point. With that kind of thinking, we will always be pushing those limits to see how much we can get away with. A child's response will be very similar when considering his behavior & attitude options if he operates from a reward and punishment system. It would be so much more positive for him to accept the need to be a responsible human being which includes making responsible decisions. That is far better

27

than choosing behaviors based on associated rewards and punishments.

I once overheard a couple of teenagers discussing their driver's license situation. These were teenagers who seemed to get some kind of traffic ticket almost weekly. They were discussing the number of points they had on their license as a result of their tickets. One was saying that he could get two more tickets for going a certain excessive speed before he lost his license. Then he explained that he could always go to a special driving school to get some of the points erased from his record. They sat there for quite some time working out all the details of how much more they could break the law before the punishment became more than they were willing to tolerate. They were considering just how far they could push the limits. There was absolutely no discussion about what was right or wrong behavior. There even seemed to be considerable pride involved in their abilities to manipulate and rebel against society's expectations. The punishment for their behavior was not nearly as motivating to them as their perceived ability to manipulate the system. They were determined to figure a way around the punishment, and to get away with breaking the law as long as possible.

By all means, help the child see the rewards of his appropriate behavior. Give special rewards for behavior that is above and beyond the call of duty. Remember that there is a time when punishment is the proper response. If someone commits a criminal act then he had better be ready for the corresponding punishment. I guess the old saying is true, "Don't do the crime if you can't do the time."

Just remember that the goal when working with kids or with families is to develop an awareness, and a system, that does not use reward and punishment as primary motivators.

BALANCE BETWEEN ACCEPTANCE AND FIRMNESS

Parents need to develop a workable balance between acceptance and firmness when it comes to their children. This is another one of those "fine lines" to watch. I know it seems like parenting involves walking a lot of tight ropes, but it is not so bad when you are aware of the basics. Every family has to decide for themselves where their lines will be drawn as far as what is acceptable and what is not. Each set of parents needs to decide for themselves how far they will go with various behaviors and attitudes. Each parent needs to decide when he will stop laughing and instead get a firm look on his face that says, "You are pushing the limits now, so be careful."

It is a natural part of the maturation process for children to challenge limits to find out what the real limits are. That is normal, healthy, acceptable behavior for a child. What is not acceptable is when they ignore or break limits that they know have already been clearly set. To break those limits is simply rebellion. They will learn how flexible limits are by how you respond to them when they are testing the limits.
If a parent laughs when a child says something that is slightly off line then he had better expect the child to come back with something just a little worse next time. Each time they are testing you to find out what your limits are. This can become a real trap for parents who are insecure about setting limits for their kids. They may find themselves acting like everything is fine, when in fact it is not.

Every counselor who ever works with kids will find this dynamic in their interactions with the kids. Every limit possible will be explored by the child over time to see what your exact limits are. By the time a child ends up in counseling, he has probably already learned to manipulate situations and people. For some kids manipulation may have become a survival technique for them, so you have to be careful about confronting that without giving them a realistic alternative. They will likely generalize that behavior, though, to virtually anyone or anything viewed as being an authority figure of any kind. Kids will want to test to see "whose side" you are on. Their willingness to participate in counseling will be adjusted accordingly. If they sense you will take either side, you have been defeated from the start. If you take the parents' side, you will be seen as the enemy. If you take their side they will lose respect for you immediately and will not listen to you. That may seem rather odd but it is very true.

Kids are usually very aware of how they are manipulating the system. They know what controls work and which ones do not. They know who to pressure, and when and how to pressure, to get what they want from someone. Believe it or not, most kids are also looking for someone who will see through their 'games' and care enough to not let them get away with it. If you take sides with the child then you will have lowered yourself to their level and so will lose their respect and your effectiveness. This is equally true for parents, counselors, teachers, or any other authority figure who hopes to earn the respect of a child. It is best to actively avoid taking sides at all. It is much more useful to frame the situation with everyone being on the same side, and working toward the same goal.

A working balance between acceptance and firmness is very important. It is valuable to consciously, and maybe even directly, state that just because you do not accept the behavior does not diminish their value as a person in your eyes.

SELF-DISCIPLINE

Discipline is a process of motivating a person to internalize principles of self-discipline. The goal of disciplining a child is to help him become self-disciplined. At first, parents make decisions for their children and use discipline to guide them in a positive direction. Part of the goal is to help the kids understand their value in the societies they are members of. They will hopefully develop a thought process that is built on a character motivated by the desire to be a productive part of those societies. They will still go out and test many limits along the way. They will even have to test their own self-imposed limits many times. It will be a proud moment for parent and child alike when they begin to make proper decisions based upon what is, and is not, appropriate behavior, and internalizing that for the future.

PARENTAL MODELING

Discipline is a learned process that adults need to model for kids. There is probably nothing worse than hypocritical parenting. If the parent is not disciplined in his own lifestyle then he is totally wasting his time trying to impress his children with the need to be disciplined. The old saying "Do as I say and not as I do" will guarantee a failed disciplining relationship with children. Do not ever underestimate the power of modeling appropriate behavior for children.

Children are always looking for someone to model their lives after. A parent had better model the lifestyle he is trying to teach his child or he is fighting a losing battle. It does not work to hope your child does not develop the habits that you demonstrate to them. To tell them to not smoke or to not drink alcohol, and then to do that yourself, is almost criminal in my thinking. To tell them to be honest and then cheat on business deals or taxes is to train them that it is acceptable to do the same. To punish them for getting home after curfew when you are rarely on time to things is to present a terrible double standard. To drop a kid off at church and then leave until you pick him up afterwards, is to tell him that going to church is not important.

I could go on and on with examples of this concept. I suspect that some parents are expressing their own frustrations with themselves when they punish or discipline their children for behaviors they dislike in themselves. You have probably heard it said that we dislike most in other people the things we dislike most about ourselves. It is good for children to learn from their parents' mistakes but they should not be expected to live a different lifestyle than what their parents model for them.

CHAPTER SIX

DISCIPLINE PRINCIPLES

In order for discipline to work, it is important to follow some specific principles. Let me suggest five basic principles that, if followed, will help the discipline process very much.

1. ENCOURAGE HONEST QUESTIONS

You will help kids understand what you are trying to teach them if you allow, and even encourage them, to ask questions. It is good for kids to know that they do not have to know everything. Lots of kids seem to be afraid to ask questions, as if that was not acceptable behavior, or that they will be seen as stupid for not already knowing the answer. It is like they are concerned about being vulnerable by admitting that they do not have the answer to a particular question.

Be careful, though, about allowing questions to turn into a game or a stalling technique. Recognize that the question "Why?" can be used as a postponing technique. Discretion is necessary. Sometimes kids will ask "Why?" not because they want to know why, but because they want to postpone what you want them to do. It is important to consider many factors in deciding how much to let children question. The point is to make sure your children know you are going to maintain an open attitude toward their concerns.

Encouraging honest questions means you have to let any honest topic be acceptable. It is also important to take and/or make the time to sit down and listen to the child's questions and do your best to help the child get the best answer possible to his question. Notice I am not saying that you need to have all the answers. I am saying that you need to sincerely listen to the questions and give your best effort to help them find the answers.

Let me encourage you also to not be too quick to give answers to questions, even though the answer may seem very easy for you. It can be a great experience to help a child research the answers to his questions. He can feel a sense of accomplishment as he develops the ability to get his questions answered in positive ways. The fact that you are part of that process will add strength to every other area of your relationship with that child as well.

Be sure to answer all questions honestly. If they trust you with their honest questions, then you should at least be willing to give them honest answers. If they find out that your answers are not reliable, then they will stop asking you for answers. Do not be afraid to tell them you do not know, if that is the case. Again, if you do not know, be sure to be part of the process of helping them find the answers.

2. EXPLAIN YOUR ANSWERS

If a child honors you by trusting you with his honest questions, then the least you can do is give him complete answers. Do not just give the facts. Talk about the values and attitudes associated with the facts. Let them pick your brain. The more they know how you think, the more open your channels of communication will be. Do not forget that goes both directions.

The more times you discuss a topic, the more you find out about each other, and the stronger your relationship can grow. When they challenge you about a discipline decision you have made, you have to be extra careful - especially if they do not agree with your decision. There will probably be times when you simply have to draw an unpopular line. Always try to explain your reasoning as well as you can in those situations. In order to do this, you will have to know the reasons yourself.

If you are making arbitrary decisions that end up controlling someone else's life, then you are setting yourself up for some tough times. Expect to be asked questions like "Why don't I get to stay up as late as my friends?", "Why don't I get an allowance as big as my friends?", "Why can't I watch that movie, or that show, on television?" Those are tough questions, and the answers may not be easy, but they are good questions that deserve good answers.

Try to avoid saying things like "I have made up my mind and that is just the way it is going to be." or "Because I said so, that's why." Those kinds of responses may end the current discussion, but will also end what could have been many other positive discussions in the future.

I worked with one family that had their communication process come to a complete stop over the issue of trust. The child expected his parent to trust him even though much of his behavior demonstrated that would not be wise. He opened our discussion by defiantly stating about his mother "She does not trust me, she is just stupid." When he said that, he looked me directly in the eyes, as if trying to intimidate me into defending his honor. I returned his gaze directly and simply stated "Based on the history of your behavior, I do not trust you either. I would like to trust you though. I hear your words saying you want to be trusted. I would be glad to help you develop the kind of lifestyle in which people can trust you, if you would like me too." My response did not take sides even though it would have been easy to do in that case. His argument was diffused. He was offered an opportunity to make an honorable decision. His value as a human being was not challenged. His mother and I were both amazed at his favorable response. In reviewing the history of the situation with them in future discussions, he shared how defensive he felt when, even though it was ultimately true, his mother put labels on him like liar, cheater, etc.

When I told him the truth without labeling him it did not diminish his need to accept responsibility for his own behavior. It just opened up avenues of communication in the process. In one of our discussions the mother expressed frustration because she felt guilty for not trusting him. She thought she had to trust him because he was her son. When she shared that information with him his attitude almost instantly softened towards her. He even volunteered the fact that it is no sin for a parent to not trust a child if the behavior does not merit that trust.

All of these positive discussions, and ultimately some impressive changes in behaviors and attitudes, resulted from them sharing their true thoughts with each other. It changed from a power struggle to a cooperative effort because they had learned new ways to communicate their inner thoughts and feelings with each other. One of the main benefits of sharing our thought processes with children is that they hopefully can learn practical and sensible ways to think through their challenges. It can give them good practice on how to make conscious, quality decisions instead of just impulsively bouncing through life.

3. EXEMPLIFY CONSISTENCY

Children are often robbed of trust for their parents when the parents use "hit and miss" methods of discipline techniques. If you discipline one way one time, and another way the next time, then you are not being consistent. This is an especially important thing for parents to discuss with each other so they can be sure they are consistent with their children.

Spouses need to come to an agreement about what the standards and rules of the home are going to be. Character qualities and rules the children are expected to live by need to be consistent with what they see in their parents. Rules need to be enforced in a way that is clearly predictable to the child.

Discipline processes in your home should not be a mystery. When a messy room is ignored one time, and severely punished another time, the parents are asking for trouble. If the family understands that certain behaviors are acceptable or unacceptable, then responses to those behaviors should be consistent.

STAIR-STEP DISCIPLINE

Talking about being consistent does not mean that there cannot be levels of consequences for behaviors. In fact, I usually encourage families to develop a stair-step process of discipline for each family member, and then to be consistent with its enforcement.

Children need to understand that a small rule consistently ignored produces a large issue. It may start out a small issue, and call for small consequences, but the consequences grow in severity as the rule is repeatedly ignored. I like to have each member of a family write out what they perceive the family expectations of them are. That includes specific chores they are responsible for, as well as what attitudes and behaviors are expected of them. I then have them list with each of those expectations what the consequences are when they are not met. I give them a week or so to do this and ask them to not let any other family member see what they have written. Then during our next discussion we compare what everyone wrote. It is amazing how little agreement these papers usually have. That makes it really easy to show them that they really do not have a clear idea of what is expected of each other. It should not be very surprising, then, that they have lots of arguments about those things.

As we discuss expectations together, we begin to develop a consensus of what the household expectations will be. Since they all work on this together, the final product will contain no surprises. Many future arguments are averted because they all had a part in developing the plan. When we have the final product developed, we go through each one and discuss what the consequences should be when those expectations are not met. We discuss what the motivators are for each of the family members. From that list, then, we develop a progressively more severe list of consequences for repeated breaking of the rules.

FAMILY MEETINGS

The next step is to develop a regular schedule of family meetings to discuss how things are going. Changes to their family agreement can only take place during a family meeting so everyone is involved in the process. This also makes the best time to discuss things like what to do with vacation time or deciding other things that impact the whole family. These meetings should be scheduled for the same time each week so everyone can plan ahead to be there.

Making these meetings of ultimate family importance helps families develop a commitment to each another. Only extreme situations should ever excuse anyone from the meeting.

The chairmanship of the family meeting can rotate through each family member so no one feels left out of the process. The family meeting can also help the family avoid arguments in between meetings. If there is a problem concerning discipline during the week, it becomes very easy to simply add that topic to the agenda for the next meeting. Many arguments can be avoided through that process. All chores of the family are listed during these meetings. Chore assignments are then given to the proper person during the meeting. The chores can be reassigned on a predetermined time schedule so people get some variety along the way. It is nice to know that you will not be stuck with the worst chore "for the rest of your life." Knowing that an undesirable job will only last for a certain period of time increases the likelihood of its being done well, and without complaints of unfairness.

There is another positive about this whole process. When each person has been a part of, and even approved, the development of the levels of discipline for the family, then the whole discipline process will likely be perceived in a much more positive way. When they are choosing their behaviors, they are also choosing for themselves what consequences they can expect for inappropriate behavior. That defuses the power struggles so many families have.

The parent does not have to be the "heavy" in the whole process. It becomes a simple response of "When you chose to participate in that behavior, you also chose the consequence that you yourself had a part in determining." Negotiation is not allowed at that point. The consequence for that action is non-negotiable. If they want to adjust the consequences for future occasions of breaking that rule then they can put it on the agenda for the next family meeting. It is a good idea to put an "Agenda Board" on the refrigerator, or somewhere else handy, for everyone to use. They can add to the list when the subject is fresh on their minds so they do not have to worry about forgetting it before the next meeting. This whole process can seem rather cumbersome at first. It would be a good idea to ask for the help of a good family therapist during the first couple of meetings. You do not have to accomplish everything during the first meeting. You could spend one whole meeting just talking about the items that need attention for future meetings. Make an outline of the things I have mentioned and develop a schedule to have them completed.

Families typically end up enjoying the process of these family meetings when they see how well they work. They are doing specific things geared to helping the family. Their input is requested, discussed, and honored. It is easy for them to begin to feel that things really can improve in their family situation, and that they will be respected in the process.

Whenever you start putting order to disorder, there will likely be an accompanying feeling of excitement and hope. For many families these discussions gave them the first hope they had felt in a long time. I have worked with many parents who really did not have any idea of how to be an effective parent. They were raised in dysfunctional families themselves. They had a hard time believing that things could ever improve. It is good to encourage the parents to also be involved in parenting classes at the same time so this process can be strengthened.

At this point perhaps I should remind you that being consistent does not mean you have to be perfect. No one has achieved perfection as a parent, and I doubt you will be the first one. Besides, if you were perfect, you would be boring.

One of the downfalls of being human is that you simply may not be in the proper state of mind to sit down and have an in-depth conversation about your thought processes related to a family challenge. (In other words, you just do not feel like talking.) You may be feeling angry at the time and know that you just would not be a good talker at the time. The situation is compounded if your anger is directed at that child and he wants an immediate explanation of your anger. It is important to try not to avoid discussions just because you are not in the mood at the time. If you feel like you might do more harm than good by talking right then, it is all right to wait awhile. Say something like "I know you want to discuss this with me, and I am willing to talk about it, but I need a little time alone right now." At that time it is good to set a specific time when you will talk. You can agree to talk about it in 30 minutes or an hour. Try to make it as soon as possible. Try to never let a discussion be put off until the next day. You being consistent does involve practicing self-control and choosing your reactions to your children's behavior. You have an excellent opportunity to model appropriate emotional and behavioral control when you are dealing with some tough feelings. Your child may even be testing you to see how you are going to react. If you are consistent under those circumstances then your request for them to be consistent has much more validity.

4. ENFORCE RESTRICTIONS

Every one of us has a potential for being very selfish or very good. Of course the good part should be encouraged above the selfish part. Restrictions placed upon us play an important part in molding our potentials. Restrictions are not placed on children for the purpose of embarrassing, sheltering, or irritating them.

Wise parents know that temptations can sometimes be overwhelming. Restrictions are assigned to help them resist those temptations.

NEGATIVE RESTRICTIONS

As parents deal with their children's behavior, they run the risk of becoming overly restrictive. Restrictions should not ignore personal liberty or limitations. You cannot deny a child the chance to cope with the world. In the long run it does not solve anything by restricting the child to the house all the time. They must consistently have the opportunity to discover what current expectations their society has of them and to make personal adjustments by functioning in that society. The most positive approach is to help the child sort through his thinking relative to those expectations. Do not try to make all of those decisions for him. He may make some decisions that are not very positive but will learn a great deal through the process. Help him see what options may be available to him. Let him make the decisions that he is capable of making. Allowing him to make some decisions, while helping him understand the possible consequences of those decisions, is much more productive than making all of those decisions for him. The goal of this process is to help the child make positive decisions in his life. If you make all of their decisions for them, they will not learn the process for themselves. Let them make some decisions that are not life-threatening so they can learn to make good decisions for themselves.

POSITIVE RESTRICTIONS

I do believe it is true that children really do want limits to be set for them. They may complain at times when they do not agree with a limitation placed on them, but that does not mean they do not want, and need, limitations. Restricting a child does not imply a lack of trust in the relationship. Restrictions simply acknowledge that we recognize that human emotion, logic, and will are vulnerable to certain temptations. This is especially true for kids who are still discovering and setting priorities and motivations for their lives.

When you tell your child that you want him home by midnight you may get a response something like "Oh mom, you do not trust me or you would let me stay out longer." That can be a very persuasive argument. You may be tempted to feel guilty for wanting him to come home at that time after you hear such an argument. Instead of feeling guilty I might suggest a response of "Yes, I do trust you, but I also trust the temptation and the power of many of the things that go on out there after midnight. I am not mistrusting you, but I know that right now you do not need to be put in that situation." That kind of response allows you to be consistent in discipline without attacking the child's reliability.

Realize also that the restrictions placed on a child should depend on the age and maturity level of the child and the circumstances. Do not be shaken when a child complains that you are restricting or disciplining him differently than you did his older brother or sister. They may even pull out the big guns by telling you how unfair that is.

Do not be afraid to treat your children as individuals instead of simply clones of their older siblings. If you are careful to respect and treat each child as an individual then you can more easily discipline in an individual fashion. Your child is probably being very challenged by peer pressure. I would encourage you to consistently reinforce the concept that he is an individual before he is part of a group so he must do what he knows is right when he feels pressured by others to do something else.

LIFE IS NOT FAIR

Someone once said, "Life is not fair, get used to it!" Like it or not, that is a true statement. It is very important to help your children realize that life is not fair. But that doesn't have to be such an awful thing if you put it into the proper perspective. If they expect life to be fair, they will be forever disappointed. There will always be someone who gets more and someone who gets less. There will always be

41

times when the supply runs out and the rest of the people in line have to do without.

People who expect life to be fair will likely end up very bitter people as they experience some of the unfairness of life. Most people do not mind life being unfair as long as they are on the receiving side, but get very upset when they are on the other side.

5. EXPECT FAILURES

Allow for failures as you discipline. Developing the ability to learn from mistakes helps develop good character. Mistakes are an inevitable part of everyone's life. We grow stronger by learning not only what to do, but also by learning what not to do. Both sides of that are often best learned through personal experience. It is nice if we can learn from other people's mistakes but there is nothing like a lesson learned from personal experience. That does not mean that every person has to relearn all of the lessons of life that generations past have already learned. It just means that it is all right to make mistakes once in awhile as long as you learn from them. The worst thing is to continue to make the same mistake over and over again without learning from it. Some people seem to think they can continue to do things the same way but get different results - it just does not work that way.

A BAD CASE OF "PARENTAL MOUTH"

I have coached virtually every age of kid in virtually every sport in existence at one time or another. There are times when I have wanted to call time out and deliberately go over to the bleachers and strangle a parent. The child is out there on the playing field doing his very best. He wants desperately to have his parent be proud of what he is doing out there. Instead the parent is sitting in the bleachers yelling at the kid for every little thing that is not done perfectly. I have heard parents yell out, for everyone to hear, things like "Can't you do anything right?" or "You'd better never do that again." There is no other way to describe behavior like that except to say it is cruel and thoughtless. It certainly is not correction or discipline. Parents like that are just demonstrating their own insecurity and insensitivity, and need some discipline, or maybe even some punishment, of their own.

Do not use an opportunity to make a correction as a time to tear down or belittle. Some people seem to feel better about themselves as they demean someone else, as if that makes them superior in some way. In reality, it demonstrates the exact opposite. Children certainly do need correction. The pain, confusion, and guilt of failure, however, should never be used to humiliate them or to crush their spirit. It is terrible to do it in public, but it is just as bad to do it in private.

THE POWER OF PREDICTION

I have found in my counseling that there is a tremendous power of prediction that can be incredibly helpful and encouraging. I have often set down with parents and predicted likely behavior patterns to expect from their children as the counseling process progresses. So often a parent will see it as a total failure when their child repeats an inappropriate behavior that had supposedly been extinguished. When they see old behaviors being repeated, they are tempted to think very fatalistically, and conclude that they might as well just give up even trying. In other words, they tend to expect perfection from their children as the counseling process progresses.

To expect anyone, and especially children, to not mess things up along the way is just not realistic. When I am talking about this with the parents I predict a certain amount of "failure" along the way. I almost set them up to even expect things to go wrong once in awhile. This becomes very positive when things do indeed go wrong. Instead of seeing that as a sign of failure, they can instead see it as a predictable part of the change process. The accuracy of their predictions gives them a sense of control even though situations are occurring that formerly indicated that things were out of control. I point out that anything that can be predicted can also be prepared for, and consequently handled in a well-planned way.

With good planning, those negative times are not disabling like they used to be. I suggest that instead of expecting perfection it might be a better goal to try to gradually lengthen the time between negative times until the positive times become prominent. I have been amazed at what a comforting and realistic approach this has been for families.

CHAPTER SEVEN

BEHAVIOR CHARTS

I think this would be a good place to suggest an alternative to all of the yelling and screaming that takes place in so many homes every day. How many of you have felt very frustrated because your child did not seem to be willing to follow your instructions any more? How many of you have felt like you were losing control? Yes, I see your hands going up! Lots of people have experienced those thoughts and feelings. Many have literally screamed at their kids until they had no voice left - but with little or no positive result. All the threats, warnings, and promises didn't work. Well, I offer you here a way to stop being the "heavy."

I have helped many parents implement a behavior chart that has been very helpful. The chart has expected behaviors and attitudes clearly outlined on it. In addition, the chart has a list of things that are positive motivators to the child. i.e. playing with friends, playing their computer or video games, watching TV, talking on the phone, etc. Those motivators are arranged from the least motivating to the most motivating, and may change from week to week due to new motivators that are unique for that week (like a party this weekend, or something like that).

The chart reflects the days of the week and covers a period of time that is appropriate for the child. Time means less to a younger child so the chart would likely cover only one day. Older children understand the concept of time so the chart can cover a longer period of time. A chart covering a period of one week is appropriate for most older children. The parent simply puts a check mark on the chart each time an undesirable behavior or attitude takes place. After a pre-defined number of 'grace' checks each day (usually one or two), every subsequent check mark means that the next item on the motivation list is lost for one week.

My intent with this chart is to replace arguing and power struggles with respect and dignity. Since the child knows exactly what the expectations are, and what the consequences will be for not following them, he cannot complain when he ends up experiencing the consequences of his choices. I teach the parents to very calmly say something like "I don't understand why you would choose to get a check mark for that behavior, but I will honor your choice."

It is amazing how quickly the child will learn that his choices have consequences - and he is in control of those consequences. It very rapidly removes the need for any power struggles because nobody has to be in a position of arbitrarily having to impose consequences after they lost the power struggle. I encourage the parents to not raise their voices, to not threaten or warn of an upcoming check mark if a certain behavior continues, to not participate in any kind of power struggle whatsoever. I encourage them to simply very calmly honor their child's choices.

It is amazing how soon most children begin making better choices for themselves since they can immediately see the direct correlation between their choices and their privileges. It is often almost humorous to watch a child struggle with his choice of whether to talk back and lose a privilege, or to save his privileges by doing what he is supposed to be doing. I also caution the parents to understand that they must model the proper attitudes they are expecting from their children.
The chart should include three parts:

1. A LIST OF WHAT EXPECTATIONS THE CHILD IS REQUIRED TO MEET

This list should include the attitudes and behaviors that everyone in the family is expected to meet. It is important to be very specific with these so there are no loopholes. I tell parents to operationally define their expectations - that means that they are not subjective, but very objective, able to be measured. Examples might be:

a. We will speak to one another with a calm, respectful voice.

b. When someone speaks to you, you will acknowledge their communication. Once you have acknowledged the communication, you will be held accountable for the content of that communication.

c. You will take out the trash before you go to school on Tuesdays. Taking out the trash includes emptying all trash baskets from all of the rooms upstairs into the trash containers being taken outside.

d. You will discontinue using the Game boy/X-Box/etc. within 5 minutes of being told to stop. The extra five minutes acknowledges that you may not be in a part of the game where you can easily turn it off without losing hard earned progress, so it gives you a chance to finish the level you are on and/or save the game before turning it off.

e. You will be certain that all of your clothes that need washed be placed in the laundry basket (not around it) the night before designated laundry days.

f. You will complete your chores as outlined on the chores sheet according to the schedule posted.

Etc. Etc.

That is just a sample list. Be certain that your list includes the specifics of any individual and house rules that you expect to see followed. This may be a rather long list for some families but that is OK. People always tend to function better in an environment that clearly defines its expectations. Any behavior or attitude that is not responded to appropriately on the list must then result in a check mark being placed on the chart. You are not needing to punish them. You are just honoring choices made.

2. A LIST OF THINGS THAT ARE MOTIVATORS FOR YOUR CHILD

The motivations should be listed in order of importance, from the least important to the most important. Examples might be:

a. Using the telephone.

b. Watching television

c. Staying up past 9:00 at night

d. Going to the park with friends after school.

e. Playing video games

f. Chatting with friends online

g. Checking and writing E-Mails

h. Going to the party on Friday night

i. Using the car

   Etc. Etc.

3. THE CHART ITSELF

The chart usually covers a one week period of time for older kids, and a smaller amount of time for younger children. For example:

BEHAVIOR CHART FOR MICHAEL FOR WEEK OF NOV 3 - 9, 2003						
Monday	Tuesday	Wednesday	Thursday	Friday	Saturday	Sunday
In squares below, write the number of which privilege was lost, what day it was lost, and when the privilege will be restored. (Normal time for privilege loss is one week.)						

Your child always has the right to ask for an explanation if he does not agree with a check mark he was given - but he must do it at a time, and with an attitude and voice tone, that is seeking understanding instead of complaining.

A scenario could go something like this: Michael has been playing a computer game for about an hour. You tell him he needs to stop now and take a shower. Michael acknowledges that he heard you. (You haven't effectively communicated your instructions until they have been acknowledged.) Ten minutes later you return to find that he is still playing. You do not remind him that you asked him to get off the computer. You do not warn him that he is going to get a check mark if he doesn't get off right now. You do not raise your voice, or count to three, or any of the other techniques that so many parents use - those techniques just teach the child that he doesn't need to respect and act on your instructions the first time because you will enable his disobedience by repeating yourself several more times. I wonder how many kids have learned that they really do not need to do what they are told until the tone or volume of their parent's voice reaches some subjective, but ominous, level.

At that point, you simply very calmly state: "I do not understand why you would choose to get a checkmark, but I will honor your choice."

49

If he responds by complaining, and trying to justify his disobedience, you simply repeat your new mantra: "I do not understand why you would choose to get a checkmark, but I will honor your choice." and give him another checkmark. You can be sure he will be counting the cost of continuing to try to justify himself. At first you may find yourself giving quite a few checkmarks, and consequently he will be choosing to lose quite a few privileges, but you will be surprised how quickly that usually changes. It is amazing how quickly even the most rebellious of kids begins to find some pride in having very few checkmarks at the end of the week. He has learned that the number of checkmarks, and consequently his number of privileges, is a result of his choices, instead of a result of being able to win a power struggle with his mother.

If he disagrees with a checkmark, he can choose to come to you (only after doing what he has been told to do) and respectfully ask you to explain why you thought another checkmark was merited so he can learn from it and consequently make wiser choices in the future.

It might be a nice thing also to establish an extra positive for the whole family if your child completes the week with fewer than a predetermined number of checkmarks. You might, for example, agree to all go out for lunch together Sunday afternoon, or bowling, or anything else the family can do together if he has fewer than five checkmarks for the week. Let me encourage you to always make the positive be a family activity. You want to reinforce the idea that the greatest reward for not having discipline problems is that the family is much happier together.

CHAPTER EIGHT

COMMUNICATION TECHNIQUE

Let me be the first to admit that just having all of this information is not going to be very helpful. If you do not know how to communicate it to others then it is not going to be very useful. The world has lots of well-educated people who do not how to apply their knowledge.

Communication issues are probably the most consistent challenge to relationships of any age. People often know what they want to say to someone else but they do not know how to say it. In a family situation, where emotions may be running high at the time, this becomes an even worse problem. People end up speaking out of their emotions instead of out of their minds and so everything gets messed up. When that happens, things can often end up worse than they started. Simply knowing, and applying, the proper communication techniques would have probably made a tremendous difference.

DISCUSSION RULES

I would like to suggest some very specific guidelines to use when communicating. These are especially useful when there is a disagreement of some sort, because they will help you avoid the disagreement from turning into an argument.

The guidelines started out being called the *"Fair Fight Rules."* I have no idea who came up with the original version or I would be glad to give credit. I have seen them in so many places and written in so many ways that they may have just evolved over time from many people. These will be unique from any others, though, because I have rewritten them, added to them, and now call them *"Discussion Rules."*

Let's go through them one at a time and apply them to our topic.

1. DISCUSSIONS SHOULD BE HELD IN ORDER TO REACH A SOLUTION, NOT TO GAIN A VICTORY

We all know people who really are not interested in having a reasonable, fact-finding discussion with anyone else. They are not interested in true discussion at all. They are only interested in proving to everyone who will listen that they are by far the most intelligent person who has ever graced the face of this earth. They are so ego-involved when they talk to others that they are only motivated to impress. The only solution they can see as having any merit at all is the one they propose. All other options are to be condescended to and ridiculed.

If you are trying to gain a victory over your child, then you have already lost. No positive discussion can ensue from that premise.

Power plays and one-upmanship will only destroy any possibility of having a good discussion. You have to choose to respect the other person enough to listen to his input, and to be willing to adjust yours.

I would suggest a simple outline for finding a solution to a problem:

1. State the problem

2. Suggest some alternatives

3. Listen to any input and alternatives the other person has to offer

4. Choose an alternative

5. Implement chosen alternative

6. Discuss the results of implementing that alternative after a reasonable amount of time has passed. If the results are positive then rejoice! If the problem is still not satisfactorily resolved then you can also rejoice - because you have successfully ruled out something that does not work. Now you can go back to Step 1 and try another alternative. Repeat this process until you find an alternative that helps.

Notice that this step does not call for complaining or griping. I have had numerous people work for me in the past, and I have always made a deal with them at the beginning. I will listen to any concern they have as long as they suggest with that concern at least one positive alternative. If they do not have a positive alternative to suggest then I consider it to be just complaining, and I choose to not participate. I have used the same guideline with many of the kids I have counseled, and found it to be very successful.

That does not in any way rule out their asking for suggestions, or options, on how they might best approach a challenge. It just does not allow for gripe sessions. Parents who adopt that kind of a process often find it leads to a great deal more peace in the home.

2. YOU CANNOT REFUSE A DISCUSSION

One of the great copouts of all time is "I do not want to talk about it." Many opportunities have been lost by families who allow that to be sufficient reason to not discuss a problem. If a topic of discussion is important enough to one member of the family to ask for a discussion, then it should be important to everyone in the family. That does not mean that every discussion has to be become a big family conference. That would soon grow very old. It does mean, though, that all people involved in, or affected by, a situation should be willing to participate in a discussion aimed at solving problems related to that situation. There may be times when, because of scheduling challenges, you may need to schedule the discussion for another time. Try very hard to never make the delay time very long.

If someone asks to discuss something, and you are unable to comply right then, be sure to give a specific time in the near future when you can. Do not just say "We will talk about it later." Say "We will talk about it at 5:00 tonight" or whatever works for both of you.

Trying to talk about something when people are very angry or upset would probably not be a good idea either. It is better to schedule a discussion for later when everyone has had a chance to cool down.

3. DO NOT BE MYSTERIOUS

My original list of Discussion Rules did not include this point, but I added it when I realized how lousy I felt when someone did it to me. Do not be mysterious when you want to talk about something. It is never a good idea to go to someone and say "We have to talk" without saying what the topic of discussion will be. It may give you a feeling of control for a while, but there is an element of cruelty involved when you take such a mysterious approach. It is natural for the person to then wonder, and maybe even worry, about what it is you want to talk about. They may wonder if you are upset, or angry, about something when really you want to praise them for something. You know how miserable it can be if you have ever had your boss come up to you and say "We need to talk" and then walk away, preoccupied with something else. You spend the rest of the day wondering if you are going to get fired or get praised. If you are like most people, you will expect the worst. By the time the discussion takes place, you have probably become all defensive. You have probably run every possible scenario through your head that you could think of. You have considered all the possible defenses you could present for each possible topic of discussion. Just the words "We need to talk" imply something of great importance. Be careful to not create an urgency that does not really exist. A much better approach would be to say something like "I would like to talk to you about your thoughts concerning the price of tea in China. When would be a good time for you?" Not only will there be much less cause for anxiety, but you will be able to be much more prepared to participate in a meaningful discussion about the topic since you knew ahead of time what it was.

4. STATE YOUR PROBLEM IN THE FORM OF A REQUEST, NOT AS A DEMAND

It is always better to state things from the perspective that you have a desire to see something happen, and would appreciate the assistance of someone else. Demanding that things happen should be left for those insensitive people who are so impressed with themselves, and their sense of power, that they feel other people are just there for their convenience, and so can be ordered around.

Making demands of other people immediately, and automatically, sets up a power struggle. People are far more likely to cooperate with you when you ask for their input, rather than demanding something from them. I have seen examples where kids rebelled against structure simply because it was thrust upon them, instead of being introduced to them and then discussed. If you have to make demands to get things done by a child, then that is a good clue that there are already control issues between you.

The fastest, and surest, way to make sure a child does not do something, is usually to demand it of him. It is almost like a child cannot resist the urge to rebel against that. I say that of kids but I think it is just as true of adults. Simply adjusting the way you communicate your concern can be a big step in getting the help you need to solve it.

5. DISCUSS ONE THING AT A TIME

I have listened to people who seem to find it almost impossible to talk about one subject at a time. This can be very frustrating to someone

55

trying to discuss something. Remember Discussion Rule number one. The goal of a discussion is to reach a solution. If you cannot keep the discussion focused on that subject, then it is going to be very difficult to do any problem solving about it.

Too many times a discussion starts about one topic but by the time you quit talking you cannot even remember what that topic was. Every possible tangent has been explored, and nothing is accomplished. It is like running a verbal maze that has no end. All you know is that you walk away frustrated, and with no fewer problems. Children can become masters at leading a discussion away from its intended course, so be careful to not enable their misdirection efforts.

It amazes me that there are teachers and parents who still fall for that trick. I have been both the student and the teacher when "the tactic" was employed. I can remember times in school when we would deliberately get a teacher off on a tangent in order to avoid a particular topic of study. It worked embarrassingly well. Kids know exactly what topics are effective to use to change the subject of a conversation with their parents. Do not be afraid to say "Wait a minute, that is not the topic we are discussing right now. We can talk about that subject also if it is truly important to you, but first we need to finish this topic."

6.   IF THE DISCUSSION IS A MATTER OF FACTS, MAKE SURE YOU HAVE THE FACTS.

Too many parents, teachers, bosses, and others spend their times being detectives. It is not necessary to be a detective. What is important, though, is that if you accuse, or imply, that someone did something wrong, you had better have your facts straight first.

Do not ever accuse someone of something unless you can back it up with solid facts. I have seen so many families get into terrible arguments because the parent accused the child of doing something,

56

and the child denied it. Then the parent spends the next few days playing detective and trying to build a case to support the accusation. The relationship can only be harmed by such distrust.

If you have concerns about something, or even suspect something, do not make accusations. Call for a discussion and talk about your concerns in a non-accusatory manner. Ask for input. If they deny it, then leave it at that until you can support your concerns with fact. There are lots of kids who will continue to deny when you catch them red-handed, but then at least you know the facts and can respond accordingly.

One time I was counseling with a married couple from out of town who were having a tremendous argument. The wife was accusing the husband of going somewhere she did not think he should be. She even accused him of being unfaithful to the marriage by being out with another woman at the same time. He vehemently denied the accusations. (There was no evidence of infidelity from him in the past either.) He repeatedly stated that he had been at the library reading a certain book. He told her the title of the book he was reading, where he sat, and what hours he was there. The wife went on and on verbalizing her anger and even threatened to leave him because she was so sure he was lying. Finally, I decided to make a telephone call to the library since it was a small town and I knew the very elderly librarian. I put the conversation on speaker phone so the couple could hear everything that was said. I asked the librarian if any out-of-towners had been to the library earlier that day. (Small town librarians know those things.) She shared the exact story the man had told of being in the library. She knew the name of the book he read, where he sat, and the exact time he was there. (Such an exciting life this librarian had.) Her story and his story were identical. Well, the wife had to do some serious back-peddling when the truth was confirmed. She had created an incredible scene and a lot of misery for herself because she made an accusation without having the facts. That scene is played out between parents and children in many homes every day. Accusations without the facts destroy relationships.

It is fine to talk about opinions, but make sure they are presented that way. Do not present an opinion as a fact.

7.   DO NOT ALWAYS EXPECT EVERYONE TO AGREE WITH YOU

It can be very healthy to have a diversity of opinions. Life would be boring if we all agreed with each other. I suspect that a very high percentage of arguments result from one person trying to get another person to think the same as himself. There are typically many different ways to look at any particular topic. That diversity is fine as long as morality or safety are not compromised. If you are having a discussion that is based upon an opinion, recognize it as just that.

The goal of parenting is not to create a family of adolescent clones. The goal is to create a family of individuals capable of considering options related to a challenge, and making quality decisions based on positive, moral thought processes. You do not always have to agree with your child. Maybe the opposite of that statement is even more important. Your child does not always have to agree with you. Sometimes it can be very healthy to disagree. Sometimes the best you can do is agree to disagree. You may get someone to "agree" with you just to shut you up. It reminds me, though, of a saying that says, "A man convinced against his will is of the same opinion still."

8. DO NOT TRY TO MIND READ. ASK INSTEAD.

A smile comes to my face as I consider the many people who seem to think psychologists and other counselors can read minds. I have had people become strangely silent when they find out that I am a Licensed Mental Health Counselor. They invariably ask me if I am analyzing everything they are doing and saying. I have actually been asked before if I could read peoples' minds. "No," I calmly tell them. "And neither can you."

When was the last time you heard someone say something like "I know why you did that." or "You did that just to make me angry." Well, maybe they were right. And maybe they were wrong. To set yourself up as a mind reader, though, is a very precarious position to be in. You may know someone well enough to have a very good idea of their motivations and thought processes, but that still does not excuse you to set yourself up as a mind reader. It will nearly always be a more productive approach to ask the other person what he is thinking, or why he did something.

Do not be one of those parents who proclaims his incredible wisdom and mind reading power while perched on your lofty throne of parenthood. Acting like you know what is going on in another person's head is a quick way to assure that person will stop volunteering to have conversations with you. The next time you are tempted to say "I know what you are thinking," change it to something like "You seem to be deep in thought. Is there anything you would like to talk about? I care and I can be a good listener." That response will likely be far more effective after your child recovers from his shock.

9. DO NOT OVER-GENERALIZE

Have you ever been really irritated when someone used generalizations in their discussions? Generalizations are the soil in which prejudices and other untruths grow into social disasters.

When you say a generalization like, "That is just the way teenagers are," you are doing a tremendous injustice to the many teenagers who are not "like that." This goes back to the discussion about the danger of using labels. How many arguments, fights, and even wars, have occurred because someone decided a whole race of people, or a certain group of people, were all a certain way? Words like always, never, all, nobody, everybody, etc. usually indicate a generalization, so be careful with those words.

To generalize when communicating about your children, their personalities, their motivations, their friends, or other such things, is to set yourself up to be alienated from your child. Do your best to understand and accept the individuality of each of your children as you attempt to have discussions with them. They will respond much better to your efforts and very quickly confirm that individuality to you.

10. DO NOT ASSUME OR JUMP TO CONCLUSIONS

Be very careful about assuming that you know what is happening with your child. It is so tempting to make decisions based on very little information. Too often our assumptions spring from our own personalities and motivations. I think of some past arguments and hurt feelings that I could have avoided if I would not have made an assumption, or jumped to a conclusion. When was the last time you assumed your child was "up to something" because he was acting suspicious or had an unusual mood? When was the last time you made an inaccurate accusation because you assumed something was true that you later found out was not?

Learn to listen to yourself as you are having a discussion so you can avoid voicing an assumption that may or may not be true. Even better, learn to think through what you are saying before you say it.

11. DO NOT DIG THINGS OUT OF THE PAST

Do not dig things out of the past. To dig things up about a person's past, and use it against him, is definitely dirty pool. Leave the fossils of the past to be studied by the archaeologists. I know people who almost seem to keep a log of past behaviors or conversations to use as artillery in their next argument. I do believe it is true that the best predictor of future behavior is past behavior, barring some significant intervening event. That does not, however, excuse throwing past behavior up in a person's face in a discussion. I sometimes call this the "Yeah, But" Syndrome. You know the process. One person says "You were wrong when you did that behavior." The accused person then comes back with the less than brilliant response of "Yeah, but you did this behavior so who are you to talk?" After the verbal fencing is complete, and those involved have been reminded of their every past indiscretion, the discussion ends with everyone angry, and nothing positive being accomplished.

Now, with all of that having been said, it is important to be aware of a balancing factor. A child will be quick to challenge you about reminding him of his past when he becomes aware of these rules. This rule is not meant to enable a person to avoid responsibility for past behaviors. There are times when past behaviors continue to be part of the present also. When a problem has not been resolved, and continues to occur, then it is very appropriate to discuss the history of that behavior, and what your response will be if that behavior continues. If what is happening today is a continuation of what happened yesterday, then yesterday is not yet history. This rule is meant to let bygones be bygones, not to avoid responsibility.

12.   DO NOT MAKE SPEECHES

Have you ever tried to talk to someone who never seemed to breathe while they were talking? They just talk in one non-stop flurry of words? They seem to talk in paragraphs, or chapters, instead of sentences. Even if you wanted to say something, you probably could not get a word in edgewise. More likely, though, you are probably trying to find a way to get away from them. People who talk in paragraphs or chapters, instead of sentences, are never much fun to talk with because they seem to be talking "at" you instead of "with" you.

Virtually every language on the face of the Earth uses the period as one of its most important punctuation marks. We would do well to use lots of periods in our discussions. If you are like the person who talks until he stumbles upon something valuable to say, you will likely soon discover yourself all alone. No one else will want to talk to you. By the time you get to the end of a discussion with a speech-maker, you will probably have forgotten what the discussion started about anyway.

Decide what you have to say and say it. Then close the mouth and purpose to listen to what the other person has to say. If you are talking more than the other person, you may be talking too much. This is especially important when you are talking to your children. They will soon learn to ignore you when you are talking, and communication will come to a halt. I have gone so far as to give speech makers an assignment to limit the number of words they can use in a sentence. It has bordered on comical to watch some people trying to comply with an assignment to limit the length of their sentences to 7-10 words, and then pause for a response from the other person. The point is quickly made though.

13. NEVER INTERRUPT - LISTEN TO THE OTHER PERSON

I think God was making a point when He only gave us one mouth but gave us two ears. Consider your listening skills. Are you one of those people who is always finishing other people's sentences for them? Are you concentrating on your next statement while someone else is trying to say something to you? Are you looking for an interrupt spot so you can share your wisdom? Not only is this a very selfish discussion style, but it is also very ineffective. When you do those things you are telling everyone around you that what you have to say is more important than what the other person is saying. Ultimately the message is also that you are more important than they are. If you are like that with your children you will soon see them discontinue any efforts to share their thoughts with you.

Listen with all of your attention. Value what they are saying and respond accordingly. They are much more likely to share their thoughts with you if they know you value what they are saying. That is just one more way to let them know that they are valuable to you.

14.   NO NAME CALLING

This is a very basic rule that we have already alluded to in several other places. Do not label people. Be very careful to not tell your children what "irresponsible little brats" they are. Do not ever tell them their serious questions, thoughts, or discussion inputs are stupid, or a waste of time. Always go back to the need your children, and others, have to know they are valued. That includes what they have to say.

15.   NO EMOTIONAL BLACKMAIL

We probably all know people whom we can totally shut down in conversation by saying just the right words in just the right way. A classic is the statement "If you really loved me you would do what I want." Or "If I was really important to you, you would not act that way." Those kinds of statements are nothing short of emotional blackmail. They are meant to carry the sting of personal rejection. They are meant to shut the other person up, and to hurt him in the process. They make the most fundamental accusation, and then challenge him to prove it wrong by his behavior.

Children can be very good at using this weapon. Adopted children often know they can inflict pain by saying something to their step-parent like "You are not my real parent, so I do not have to take that from you." If children know they can control you with those kinds of statements, they will use them unmercifully.

Children are not the only culprits though. I have heard many parents use the same kinds of statements against their children. It is almost like those statements are held in reserve to use when nothing else seems to work. If they can get their children into a mode of having to prove their love for the parent by doing certain behaviors, then they are in a powerful position. What they may not realize, though, is that deep down inside there is probably a seed of resentment, and maybe even hate, growing in the child.

Emotional blackmail is one of the most cruel things a person can inflict upon another. Be careful not to do that. If you have been victimized by those statements, then it is helpful to realize that they are nothing more than emotional blackmail, and choose to not pay the extortion price.

16. YOU CAN STATE YOUR THOUGHTS IN TERMS OF BEHAVIOR, BUT NOT IN TERMS OF STATES OF BEING.

I guess I had better explain what I mean by states of being. A state of being is a feeling or emotion. It would describe what condition or state you are in emotionally. Depression is a state of being. Anger and jealousy are states of being.

Most of this book would probably be invalidated if feelings responded easily to logic, but alas, they do not. You will be relegated to a life of tremendous frustration if you try to make your feelings and emotions respond to logic. You may be able to give some intellectually logical explanation for why you are feeling a certain way, but that does not necessarily get you any closer to changing the feeling.

Telling a jealous person that his feelings stem from deep-seated feelings of insecurity and poor self-concept will not lead him to heave a sigh of relief and feel better. Telling a person he should not be depressed over a loss that you consider insignificant does not ease that person's pain. I guess discipline would be very different if feelings were logical. We could tell the angry youngster to go stand in the corner until he was happy. Of course anyone would agree that such a command would be ridiculous. And yet I have heard parents severely chastise their child for being upset as if the chastisement would change the feeling. All such a response can hope to accomplish is to heighten the feelings of despair in the child.

What you can, and should, respond to, however, is the behavior that is associated with the feeling. It is not very helpful to tell someone they should not be angry. It is very reasonable, though, to expect a child not to hit his sister, or not to slam the screen door, when he is angry. Expect appropriate behavior but be sensitive to the feelings.

17. GO BACK TO RULE NUMBER ONE AND NEVER FORGET IT - A DISCUSSION IS HELD TO REACH A SOLUTION, NOT TO GAIN A VICTORY.

IMPLEMENTING THE DISCUSSION RULES

I have had a tremendous amount of fun helping people implement these discussion rules into their lives. Most people respond with a sheltered, self-incriminating laughter, when they first see the list. I have been accused many times of writing these rules to respond to a specific person who was sitting in my office for counseling at the time.

The trick now, if we can call it that, is to have a good discussion about the discussion rules. I encourage families to sit down together and to study the rules together. Become familiar with each of them. Maybe even challenge each person to share how they see themselves, not each other, in the rules. Feel free to make adjustments to the rules if they do not quite fit your family. You may even want to add other rules that address other specific situations you are dealing with.

When you finish your discussion, agree together to abide by the rules to the very best of your ability. Try to apply the rules to any discussion you may have with people outside the family also. Use them at work, at school, and at play. Use them especially when you are going through a conflict with someone.

If you can handle the stress, it would even be good to agree as a family to help each other see how the rules are being broken. It can be lots of fun if done in the right spirit. I personally guarantee that talking with people will become much more enjoyable. Practice these rules until they become second nature to you. Other people will much more readily enter into conversations with you. People will begin to recognize that you are the one who stays reasonable when everyone else is becoming unreasonable. You will be promoted faster than anyone else, become rich beyond your wildest dreams, ... Oh all right, it may not be that dramatic, but it will surely be better than it probably is right now.

I had better warn you that bells will start to go off in your head as you become more familiar with these rules. You will just naturally start catching other people destroying their conversations because of poor communication technique. Try not to get too critical. Just smile the smile of experience and help where you can.

CHAPTER NINE

POWER AND AUTHORITY

Let's switch gears now and talk a little about what it means to have power and authority. Simply by virtue of their position, parents have a natural authority over their children. Authority, however, can be terribly abused. As many a frustrated parent will acknowledge, however, authority does not always equal power. Let me describe the difference. I may have the power to go out in the middle of an intersection and raise my hand up to stop an oncoming truck. Without the proper authority I need, however, that truck driver is not required to stop. I may quickly take my place with the last squirrel that had the misfortune of going across the street to visit the neighbors when another truck interfered with his plans.

The situation would be entirely different if I was a policeman fully outfitted in my uniform. When the truck driver saw me, he would know that he had better stop when I told him to, or be ready to pay the consequences. When power and authority are properly combined, the results are more likely to be positive.

With great clarity, my mind can hear the many parents who, with tears in their eyes, have related the frustration that comes with the powerlessness they feel with their children. Parents who may wield incredible power and authority over hundreds of people at work come home to feel terrorized by one or two young children. I suspect that every child must challenge the parents along the way in order to discover their own boundaries, but those power struggles should not become a lifestyle for the family.

Let's take a look at some of the things that many parents do that will likely lead to power struggles with their children, and some suggestions on how to respond more positively.

1. FAILING TO LISTEN TO THE FEELINGS OF CHILDREN

One of the sad things in this world today is that many people seem to have lost the ability to adequately communicate their feelings. This will be especially true of children whose parents struggle with that. It seems to be so much easier to take the "safe way" out and try to ignore feelings, especially unpleasant feelings.

If we ask someone how they are feeling, then we run the risk of them actually telling us. Then we are trapped, because then we have to respond to those feelings. The old tradition of asking someone how they are doing has become such dead words that they are usually asked with no expectation of a real response. "Fine" is the standard response, which usually means "Leave me alone and mind your own business." You will likely really catch the person off guard if you tell them a feeling when they ask you how you are doing. The truth is, though, that they will probably proceed as if you said nothing. The question usually is not asked with any intention of getting a response. The question is usually just asked out of habit, and really means nothing to the person asking it. Think of how sad that is. We have become such a fast-paced world, but at the expense of a sensitivity to the feelings of the other people in our lives.

Now consider how a younger child will perceive that kind of a response. Your child is probably right in the middle of trying to figure out who he really is in this world. He is trying to sort through a muddled mess of contradicting feelings that leaves him constantly grasping for a definition of reality.

Now more than ever, he needs someone who will help him discover his feelings without him having to beg. His words to you may seem organized enough, and not all that emotional, but he is probably hoping you can sense what is really going on inside.

There is a little bit of a Catch-22 here. If you are too quick to deal with his feelings he will likely run from you. If you do not help him express his true feelings, however, he will feel rejected and alone.

Welcome to the world of children. Maybe you can remember a time back in high school when you had a crush on someone and that other person did not even know you existed. You were devastated. You desperately wanted to talk to someone about it but were afraid they would laugh at you. So you just let the pain eat at you and fought the battle alone.

It is a fortunate, and very happy, child who has a parent who not only is sensitive enough to the child's feelings to respond to those feelings, but also wise enough to help the child discuss and work through the feelings. That parent-child relationship will be strong beyond belief if they can share their true feelings through the rough times. That will be a child who will feel very secure at home and will have much less need for power struggles or rebellion.

"I FEEL" vs. "I THINK" STATEMENTS

There is a statement that says something like "People will not care how much you know until they know how much you care."

There is a lot of truth to that. Most people are very comfortable telling people what they think. The other side of that is also very true. Most people are very uncomfortable telling people how they feel. If you do not believe that, just listen to people for a while. See how many times they start a sentence with "I think."

Most people will respond with a thought even if you ask them what they are feeling. Try asking someone how he feels about a particular issue and see how he responds. You are not likely to get a feeling, or emotion, as a response at all. Even statements that start with the words "I feel" are likely completed with a thought instead of a feeling.

I say all of that to emphasize the need for you to help your child recognize and express what he is truly feeling. You can model this by using more "I feel" statements followed by a true emotion instead of a thought.

A FEELINGS LIST

When we start a sentence with "I feel," it should be completed with a true feeling word. Here are some feeling words you might try:

-Badly	-Hateful	-Gloomy
-Agonized	-Anxious	-Apologetic
-Daring	-Mad	-Sensitive
-Awful	-Frustrated	-Silly
-Arrogant	-Bashful	-Blissful
-Moody	-Upset	-Comfortable
-Bored	-Cautious	-Confident
-Guilty	-Mixed-up	-Excited
-Determined	-Disappointed	-Disgusted
-Happy	-Ashamed	-Jealous
-Ecstatic	-Envious	-Enraged
-Strong	-Special	-Violent
-Exasperated	-Exhausted	-Grieving

-Scared	-Patient	-Caring
-Horrified	-Lousy	-Love struck
-Warm	-Loved	-Afraid
-Meditative	-Mischievous	-Obstinate
-Worried	-Sad	-Confused
-Miserable	-Optimistic	-Paranoid
-Important	-Angry	-Hurt
-Relieved	-Shocked	-Satisfied
-Embarrassed	-Understanding	-Frightened
-Sheepish	-Smug	-Sympathetic
-Shy	-Understood	-Good
-Mean	-Loving	-Sympathetic
-Discouraged	-Nice	-Brave
-Curious	-Terrible	-Funny
-Wonderful	-Encouraged	-Uncomfortable
-Different	-Aggressive	-Surprised

This is just a partial list. I have seen feelings lists with several hundred different feeling words listed. So you see, there are lots & lots of feelings we can identify in our daily lives. Have fun discovering the power of identifying and expressing your feelings, instead of just talking about what you think.

2. BELITTLING CHILDREN WITH SARCASM AND CONTEMPT

If you do not have more knowledge and more wisdom than your children, then you are in a very sad state indeed. Just your extra years of life should give you a sensibility and wisdom that children can only hope to gain as their life continues. If you feel like you have to prove your level of knowledge and wisdom to your children, then you are in trouble as a parent.

I have little patience for the parent who uses sarcasm and contempt with their children, as if that is a noble thing to do. You surrender your power over your child when you belittle what they do, say, or think. That child will likely grow to resent you. Most will eventually enter into a power struggle with you that will be very unpleasant.

I am talking about when parents say things to their children like "That is stupid," "That is really a dumb thing to do," "I thought you were smarter than that," "Can't you do anything right?", and other such statements. The child hears you saying that he is stupid. When you say things like that you are only demonstrating your own inadequacy. The child will eventually see that. When the child does realize that, your power over that child will quickly erode away.

Learn to listen to yourself. Listen for any statements that might belittle someone else and choose to leave them unsaid. Recognize them as a symptom of your own feelings of inadequacy, and work on them from that perspective.

3. EMBARRASSING CHILDREN IN FRONT OF OTHERS

I can still remember times when I felt that someone had embarrassed me in front of other people. For some reason, those kinds of situations become very strong memories in a person's life. Great harm can be done if you embarrass your child in front of his peers. This is also true if you embarrass him in front of adults, especially close relatives.

We all have large, emotional investments in how we think other people perceive us. If a parent participates in damaging those perceptions, they will quickly be seen as the enemy, and responded too accordingly. Some parents seem to think that their statements of correction will carry more impact if they are said around other people. That is true in the most negative way.

Kids can be especially merciless and cruel to each other. If you give someone ammunition to use against your child, then you had better be ready for the war. If you have something of a corrective nature that needs to be said right away, then at least pull the child aside to say it. If it can wait until you are alone that is even better. The child may never say it but he will be thankful you waited, and will appreciate you for it. That appreciation will increase your level of respect with that child which may come in really handy at a later date.

4. BEING UNFAIR OR UNREASONABLE IN THE KIND OR AMOUNT OF DISCIPLINE YOU USE

It is easy to get a little extreme in assessing consequences for your child's inappropriate behavior when you are frustrated and angry. That is why I discussed pre-planning of consequences earlier in this book. To ground a person to his room for six months for a relatively small rule infraction may seem fair to you when you would really like to box his ears in, but the end result will not be helpful. Be certain the sentence you pronounce fits the crime and is consistent with how you judge other "crimes."

If you give very strong consequences for a relatively minor rule infraction then how can you appropriately respond to something that is relatively more serious? Do not go overboard simply because you are frustrated.

5. PREVENTING CHILDREN FROM LEARNING TO MAKE THEIR OWN DECISIONS

One of the most difficult parts of parenting is in deciding where to draw the line between deciding things for your children and letting them make decisions for themselves. There are few lessons better learned than when we have to live with the natural consequences of our poor decisions. The memory of that can be very motivating the next time we have a similar decision to make.

If parents make too many of the decisions for their children then the child will not be able to benefit from the process. If you make their decisions for them then you become the bad guy any time something does not go the way they expected it too. When you feel tempted to make a decision for your child, try to turn the tables a little. Ask them what they would suggest be done in that situation. Help them explore options. Reinforce that process even if you can see that some of the options suggested are obviously not appropriate. If they suggest something positive then you have a wonderful opportunity to praise them for their wise thinking. That kind of input will be a great encouragement to them as they are faced with future challenges. Even if they make a decision that is not all that great, it would be better to let them follow through with it if you think they can learn from the process in a positive way. Of course if they make a decision that could seriously harm them in some way then you must step in and be more directive.

6. GIVING CHILDREN THE IMPRESSION THAT ACCEPTABLE BEHAVIOR IS ONLY NECESSARY WHEN AN AUTHORITY FIGURE IS PRESENT

It is almost funny to watch children, or even adults for that matter, adjust their behavior according to who is in the area. You will be doing your children a great favor by demonstrating to them, and encouraging them, to be consistent in their behavior patterns. Of course I acknowledge that we all relax in some places, and with some people, more than with others. We probably use better table manners in public than at home. We may choose our words more carefully around our boss than around a closer friend. That is very normal and acceptable behavior.

The danger, however, is that children will get the idea that they can be less responsible, or less sensitive, to people's feelings in certain settings. If they are told they should not gossip, but then hear you talking about people in an unfavorable way at home, then you are setting a poor example for them. You are basically teaching them that morality, or right and wrong, is based upon whom you are with, or where you are.

If you carry a radar detector in your car, or speed when you feel like you can get away with it, then do not be surprised when your child learns that breaking the law is all right as long as you take steps to not get caught. That is a perfect way to raise a phoney, insincere person. Your children will just as quickly learn to act one way when you are around and another way when you are not around. Remember that if a whole lot of something is wrong then a little bit of it is probably wrong also. Rarely is right and wrong defined by where you are or who you are with.

Authority is not worth much if you do not have the power to back it up. The six areas discussed in this chapter are probably the things that most interfere with a parent maintaining the proper level of power and authority needed for successful parenting. It could be a very positive move for you to sit down with your child sometime and ask

75

them how they feel about these issues in their lives. If they know you are truly trying to be aware of their feelings, then they are far more likely to cooperate with your efforts.

CHAPTER TEN

DANGEROUS THINKING

In this chapter we will take a look at some of the thought processes that children and others often have that can lead them into a great deal of trouble. A child's response to a situation will be influenced a great deal by his perspective of that situation. If he finds it difficult to accurately assess a situation then he will often find himself frustrated and frustrating. Here are some of the thought processes that will lead them in the wrong direction.

1. THINKING THAT THEIR WAY IS THE ONLY WAY

Let's face it. Some people can be incredibly self-centered. They see no problem as long as everything is going the way they want it to go. The instant things start going in a different direction though, that child will throw a fit. They live their lives as if they should get their way simply because they want it their way. If you do not fit into their plans then you are unnecessary, and therefore, unwanted.

These kids will seldom be able to function in social settings very well. They will usually be described as rebellious and unwilling to conform. The needs or desires of other people around do not seem to be important. This can be especially challenging at home because it will feel like you are in a constant power struggle with the child. Temper tantrums and threats may be commonplace. The more you try to control their behavior, the more rebelliousness you will experience. These kinds of attitudes are usually developed while the child is very young.

To let a child have his own way when he is rebelling, or having a temper tantrum, is to train the child that the likelihood of him getting his own way is directly related to the commotion he causes. These children often grow up to be angry, bitter people if their attitudes are not adjusted as children.

2. NOT BEING SENSITIVE TO THE FEELINGS OF OTHER PEOPLE

This ties in very closely with number one above. Some people seem to find it very difficult to regard other people as thinking, feeling human beings. They say things, or do things, that physically or emotionally hurt other people, but there seems to be no awareness of the damage done. They have an insensitivity to the concept of injury to others.

I once counseled a 14-year old boy who was caught stealing cars. When confronted about the behavior, he said he thought people were making a big deal out of nothing. His response was "Big deal. I didn't wreck the car and she got it back, so why should she be so upset." He had no awareness of how that person was affected by the theft of her car. It meant nothing to him when I talked about how that person's life had been violated. Further talk about trust and feelings of security fell on deaf ears. In his thinking, people and their belongings were there to be used. Respect for people and their things meant nothing to him. Of course, his response was very different if someone imposed themselves upon anything of his. His lack of ability to generalize from how he felt, with how others might feel, was incredible.

I do not intend to get on a soapbox here, but I do feel a need to discuss something I feel very strongly about at this point. I cannot help but believe that there is a strong relationship between what most kids see on television, what movies they watch at the theaters or from DVDs & video tapes, what they listen to in their music, and their thinking.

Children often spend many hours a day in front of a television watching people rape, kill, and manipulate each other. They watch the "bad guy" win battle after battle while stealing, practicing unrestrained sex, and just basically doing what he wants, while abusing other people in every imaginable way. Much of the music kids listen too not only condones, but indeed encourages, incredibly antisocial things like drug usage, rebelling against authority, suicide, and conquering others sexually. These kinds of things are glorified as the way life should be lived. When they watch and listen to those things long enough we should not be surprised when their attitudes and behaviors begin to reflect them as well. It is incredibly sad that so many parents either knowingly or unknowingly encourage their children in those negative things.

I would certainly encourage parents to decide how they want their children's attitude and behavior to be, and then compare the training they are getting through what they are watching and listening to. If the two do not agree, then they need to help their child make better decisions in those areas.

Of course this is best done while the child is very young. To wait until they are teenagers is to be asking for a major battle. To simply throw all of that stuff out one day will not likely be a very helpful approach. It will be necessary to open up some quality discussions about your concerns with your child. Be willing to listen to what your child says, but be firm about what you will allow to be watched and listened to in your home.

Remember the value of setting a consistent example for them. If you watch and listen to things you do not want them to see or hear, then do not bother talking to them about it, because your words will fall on deaf ears. Society and the movie business seems to have decided that morality is based upon how old you are. Your children will very correctly not accept that kind of thinking. They will either openly or covertly follow your lead.

3. THINKING IT IS ALWAYS THE OTHER GUY'S FAULT

I never cease to be amazed at how kids can rationalize situations around until they have totally convinced themselves that they are the victims of other people and the environment. Actually it is not fair to lay this just on kids, because a large majority of adults are guilty of the same thing.

If we can blame someone else for our feelings, attitudes, and behaviors, then we do not have to accept responsibility for ourselves. We can then hold the world accountable when we do not achieve our goals. That kind of thinking also makes failure easier to tolerate, because we think we can justify it by blaming it on someone else.

When was the last time you said, or you heard, someone else say something like "You make me so angry" or "You make me so happy"? People accept that statement as if it had some validity, which it does not.

No one else can make you angry. Our emotional responses are based upon our own personal set of thought and belief patterns. Something you get very angry about may not affect me at all. Something I get very happy about may result in you being very upset. That could only be true if our emotional responses are subjective, that is, dependent on our own personal perceptual and emotional processes.

A correct response would be something more like "When you do that I get so angry" or "When you say that I feel so happy." Life in most families would be very different if only each person understood that their emotions, and their responses to those emotions, are their own responsibility. You will emotionally be at the mercy of the world around you until you accept this truth. One of the greatest favors you can do for your child is to help him accept total responsibility for his own emotions, attitudes, and behaviors.

Virtually every child alive would admit that peer pressure is one of the most difficult things for him to deal with in his life. They will often say things like, "People make me feel so inferior." or "My girlfriend/boyfriend made me feel so jealous today." Alcoholics will often tell their spouses that they drink because of them. Those kinds of statements reveal the need to accept responsibility for themselves.

4. HAVING EXPECTATIONS OF THEMSELVES AND OTHERS THAT ARE NOT BASED ON REALITY

I am a strong believer in the power of positive thinking. I think it is great for a child to have big dreams, even dreams that are highly unlikely. To squelch a child's dream is a cruel thing to do.

Like the commercials say "A mind is a terrible thing to waste." There is a danger involved, though, that many parents seem to be unaware of. It is very important for a child to realize that most goals and dreams require hard work to achieve. Many kids expect to be the best at something without doing the prerequisite work necessary. They may have a dream of being president but not willing to do their homework or get along with other people. They may have a dream of competing in the Olympics in a certain sport but are unwilling to practice consistently.

Parents do their children a disservice by not helping them see and understand the connection between hard work and achieving goals. The result is that children often get the idea that something mystical or magical will happen along the way that will suddenly plunge them into stardom or complete success. They need to realize that success is nearly always the result of a consistent process of hard work.

5. TAKING THE EASY WAY OUT AND USING PEOPLE IN THE PROCESS

Too often children get the attitude that if something takes work to accomplish then it is not worth doing. This is different from the last point in #4 because in this case the child knows a lot of work is needed to accomplish a goal, but he is just unwilling to pay the price. They will typically have a long history of starting projects but not finishing. I know that kids are notorious for bouncing from one project to another. That in itself is normal and not a bit unusual. There is a difference with the kid I am talking about though. When you look at his projects, you will be able to see a trend in his activities. He will start a project very excitedly but when the project becomes difficult, or requires any kind of sacrifice to continue, he will quit. He does not quit because of a child-like tendency toward inconsistency. He quits because he is not willing to put any extra effort into accomplishing a goal. If that kind of attitude continues into adulthood, he will find it very difficult to maintain employment, to be a family man, or do anything else that calls for consistent effort. When his marriage or family becomes a challenge, he will simply leave it. When his boss expects more from him, he will quit.

The tendency is for this kind of person to value other people only according to how useful they are. As long as you can be seen as useful for achieving my goals, then you will be tolerated. When you are no longer useful, then you can be disregarded and ignored. You will be very disappointed if you have expectations of that person in return.

Relationships with those kinds of people are typically very one way. You are there to serve. As long as you serve without expecting anything in return, you will do just fine. The first time you let them know that you have needs too, or that you expect something from them that requires effort or sacrifice, or suggest that they are being selfish, your days as a part of their life are numbered.

6. LYING AS A WAY OF LIFE

Lying becomes a way of life for some children. It seems that some children would rather lie than tell the truth. If reality does not fit their desires, they simply lie to change it. If life as they perceive it is not exciting enough, they will lie to embellish it. Some children lie when the truth would do them better. For this kind of child, lying can become an addiction. It is as if they made a decision somewhere along the way that reality as they see it was not acceptable. They respond by living a lie. They can get caught up in a maze of lies until they themselves do not know what the truth is anymore. They lie to cover up another lie, and then lie again to cover up that lie etc. etc. This child can be very frustrating. He will lie when he is aware that everyone around him knows the truth. He will lie about his own behaviors even though he knows you are an eye witness to what actually happened. There will likely be a time when the lies all catch up with him. That time will leave him feeling very alone and empty.

Realize that this child's self-concept is probably rock bottom. He is probably convinced that if he does not lie he will not be acceptable to others. The Catch-22 he finds himself in is that he lies to make himself more acceptable to others, but his lies ultimately alienate him from those same people.

If you find any of these things happening in your child's life, you really need to talk to him about it as soon as possible. It would probably be good to have him see a professional counselor. The things we just mentioned are not minor nuisances that go away by themselves. Do not just wait, hoping your child will grow out of them. These are the kinds of things that almost always grow stronger, and more debilitating, as time goes by.

CHAPTER ELEVEN

NEGATIVE PARENTING RESPONSES

Well, it seems that up to this point we have been really rough on the kids. I guess it is only fair that we spend some time discussing specific things that parents often do that make things even worse. One of the best ways to emphasize what is most helpful is to point out what parents do that is least helpful. Do not despair if you see yourself in some of these things. There is hope.

The object of this is not to convince you of what a terrible parent you are. The object is to help you be even a better parent than you already are. So here are some parenting problem areas:

1. DENIAL

Parents seem to be really good at developing blind spots when dealing with their kids. Of course they want to believe only the best things about their kids. When negative things are happening, it is natural for their defenses to kick into high gear. (You will find a whole chapter on Defense Mechanisms in Chapter 15.) There is no devious intent. They just have a total denial of the negative that is going on.

This process is not that different from the alcoholic denying that he has a drinking problem. He really believes he is in complete control of his drinking. If someone confronts him about his drinking he will no doubt become very upset and argue very convincingly against the accusations.

This is not the same as lying. The person in denial truly believes that he is right and everyone else is wrong. They truly believe that people are making a big deal about nothing. Parents are notorious for this kind of behavior. Their denial allows them to believe that it is the neighborhood kids who do those things but "not my baby." They are blinded to the possibility that their "little angel" may be the ring leader. They tend to see everything through a filter that removes any awareness of negative relating to their child.

The child may come home with a report of negative classroom behavior from the teacher but that does not matter. His explanation that he was provoked by someone else, or the teacher was picking on him, is sufficient to exonerate him in his parent's mind. Of course during this time the child is learning that he can get away with virtually anything. He is learning that it is a very effective defense to just blame someone else for whatever is wrong.

The analogy with the alcoholic continues to be accurate at this point. The alcoholic's drinking will become progressively worse. He is likely to drink himself to death unless something so drastic happens that is so obviously drinking related that it breaks through the denial. These are always very painful times for the alcoholic as well as the family. When a child has a parent in denial, his behavior will usually follow the same pattern. He will get into progressively worse trouble until it finally becomes impossible to deny that he is indeed the one responsible.

I have counseled with many families at this stage. I have seen these kids facing consequences for behaviors including breaking and entering, armed robbery, and automobile related behavior that resulted in the death of several people. Lots of arguments have occurred when one parent is in denial and the other is not. More than a few divorces have resulted from that situation.

The following story will give you a good example of what I am talking about here. Notice the progression of Michael's behavior and his mother's denial. We can only speculate on how the story might be different if the parent had held Rodney accountable for his attitudes and behaviors from the beginning.

YOU CAN'T BLAME MICHAEL

February 1981

Michael is really fussy today. I think he's just tired. Some babies are just more fussy. Poor baby. You can't blame him.

June 1983

Michael is right in the middle of the terrible two's. It's just natural for kids to be disobedient at this age. Poor kid. You can't blame him.

April 1985

Michael just got his school shots so he's not very happy. He doesn't like the doctor anyway so he's always hard to get along with when he goes there. The doctor must have treated him badly some time for Michael to act this way in his office. Poor kid. You can't blame him.

January 1986

Michael has really become a finicky eater. I try to fix all of the things he likes but he still didn't eat anything except his dessert. I guess I'll just have to try harder to fix things he will eat. Poor kid. You can't blame him.

March 1987

Michael just wanted to play with the toy - I'm sure he didn't mean to be so rough when he grabbed it from the other kid. I don't know why that other kid couldn't share. People need to realize that Michael is just a very active kid. I don't think it is anything to get so upset about. Kids will be kids. You can't blame Michael. Poor kid.

July 1988

I'm sure Michael was just playing around when he tore those plants out of your garden. Don't worry, we'll pay for the damage. He is such a high-spirited little boy that you have to expect things like this to happen. You can't expect him to be perfect all the time. I don't want to stifle his energy. You can't blame Michael. Poor kid.

September 1990

Well, we want Michael to stand up for himself. He says those other boys started it. What do you expect when he has to fight them to protect himself? I know Michael doesn't know his own strength. I'm sure he didn't intend to hurt them that much. Of course we will pay for any doctor's bills, even though I don't think we should have to. I don't think Michael should be blamed for the fight since I'm sure he would never start a fight. We just didn't raise him that way. You can't blame Michael. Poor kid.

May 1992

I know it was wrong for Michael to say those things Coach, but he was upset that he didn't get to start in the game. I think he feels badly for behaving that way, but he couldn't help himself because he was so angry. But Coach, don't you think you share part of the blame for this too? None of this would have happened if you would have just started Michael in the game. You should expect a strong reaction from a sensitive boy like Michael when he is disappointed like that. You can't blame Michael. Poor kid.

September 1994

Why would you say something like that about Michael, Mrs. Riggle? He is such a respectful young man. I'm sure he would never treat your daughter the way she said he did. He is only fourteen years old. I know he would never use those kinds of words, especially around a girl. I doubt he even knows what those words mean. I am just going to tell Michael to stay away from your daughter if she is going to cause trouble like this. You can't blame Michael. Poor kid.

August 1995

How could you possibly think about failing Michael, Miss Cornell? I know he is way behind, but I think you give way too much homework. I know the other students are keeping up in class, but Michael is a very active kid. And you know he doesn't like doing homework anyway. So why can't you work with him better so he doesn't have all of these problems with your class? I really am getting tired of this. I don't know why everyone seems to be against Michael. We took him out of his last school because of this same sort of thing. I'm beginning to lose faith in the educational system. You can't blame Michael. Poor kid.

June 1996

How can you even say that? There is no way Michael can be the leader of that group. That group is nothing but a bunch of juvenile delinquents. Michael is a much better person than any of them. It is insulting that you would even suggest that Michael has anything to do with them. He is a good kid. I refuse to listen to any more of these accusations. Don't you have anything better to do than to stir up false rumors about my kid? You can't blame him. Poor kid.

September 1997

Michael said he was just holding it for someone else. I know he would never touch the stuff himself. We have talked to him about staying away from drugs. He was just trying to do someone else a favor so they wouldn't get in trouble. I asked Michael to tell me the truth about this so I believe what he said. He would never lie to me. I really am tired of this constant harassment of my boy. As far as I am concerned, this whole thing is over. I see no point in making this worse than it is. You can't blame him. Poor kid.

March 1998

I don't care how many people said Michael was involved. I know he wasn't. I talked with him about it and he promised me he just happened to be there when the other boys did it. I know he would tell me if he was involved. You have had something against Michael for a long time, so it doesn't surprise me that you want to hang this on him. You can't blame him. Poor kid.

February 1999

Ok, so Michael stole something from the store. It's not like he stole anything big. It was just a little thing. Haven't you ever done something like that just for kicks? I think it would be better if we didn't make a huge deal out of this. Michael says that he was just trying to make friends with some guys, and so my impressionable boy allowed himself to get caught up in the moment. Say what? It most definitely was not Michael's idea! That is a lie! Michael would never do anything like that! I will reimburse the store for everything he took, of course. We want Michael to know that we stand behind him now more than ever. You can't blame him. Poor kid.

November 2003

Yes, your Honor. I understand that this is a serious offense that Michael has been charged with. I think the whole thing is basically just a huge misunderstanding. The way I understand it, it really wasn't Michael's fault. I know him very well and ...

The story of Michael gives a very clear idea of what denial is like. Everyone see the truth except the one in denial.

2. TAKING THE EASY WAY OUT

Remember that we are talking about the behavior of parents now. It will not be helpful if the parent tries to "take the easy way out" in the area of disciplining their child. Parental failure to be firm and consistent with their children will almost always lead to many other problems.

SAYING "YES" WHEN YOU SHOULD SAY "NO"

A good example of this is when parents say "Yes" to their child when they really want to say "No." They just know that if they say "No," they are going to have an argument on their hands. They may have had a long day at work, or have other things on their mind. They are more motivated to avoid an argument than they are to provide consistent parenting to their child.

The child will quickly learn how to manipulate his parents to get what he wants. He probably learned a long time ago that he will get his way as long as he argues with you long enough. He knows that he can wear you down, and finally get his own way.

It is easier to say "Yes" than to deal with the real problem of a rebellious child. You may say "Yes" sometimes when you know you should say "No." To say "No," though, would interfere with your own schedule. So your responses to your child become a matter of personal convenience instead of conscientious parenting.

Your child will learn that it is best to ask you for things when you are busy, because then he is more likely to get his own way. You may avoid a scene right then, and your child may seem to be happy with you at the time, but you are asking for far larger problems later.

DOING YOUR CHILD'S WORK FOR HIM

Another example of taking the easy way out is when you do things for your child that he really should be doing himself. After all, it is probably easier sometimes to clean the child's room for him than going through the challenge of getting him to clean his own room. He will patiently listen to you as you make martyr statements like "I have to do everything around here." He knows that it is just a waiting game. If he waits long enough, you will do his work for him. He knows he may have to put up with your yelling and screaming in the process. That is a small price to pay, though, as long as you end up doing his work for him.

I have been a teacher long enough to see a lot of homework that was obviously done by the parents. I know the parent thinks they are doing their child a favor by "helping" him, but the exact opposite is true. It is great for a parent to encourage their child in the homework process, make sure the child has enough time and a suitable environment to do it well, and even to work with them at times to help the child solve especially difficult challenges. But it is totally counter-productive when the parent does more of the work than the child. When the parent does more than they should, they are fostering a dishonest and cheating environment, not only in relationship to homework, but anything else that the child may find difficult along the way. This is just as true when the parent does most of a Science Fair project, or building a Cub Scout Pinewood Derby car, or anything else like that.

LETTING YOUR CHILD BE A QUITTER

It is also taking the easy way out when you let your child be a quitter. This does not diminish the acknowledged value of letting your child try different things until he finds something he is willing to invest his energies in. The problem comes when a child learns from a parent that if something takes a little extra effort, and you do not feel like expending that energy, then it is all right to quit. The child will learn that the value of something diminishes as the amount of effort it takes increases.

It is a great disservice to allow your child to quit things just because the going gets tough. That might make it easier for you at the time, but in the long run you will regret it. Please be aware that this

91

includes the amount of effort you are willing to exert in order for your child to pursue some of his goals.

I know you can only be in so many places at once, and that you have other priorities as well. Too many parents, though, will not allow their child to be involved in something because it means some extra trips in the car, or because it might interfere with something else. Decisions like those are often tough decisions. Be careful to not make those decisions simply based on what is the easiest, or most convenient.

3. FAILURE TO DEMAND ACCOUNTABILITY & TRUSTWORTHINESS

You are not demonstrating trust in a child when you never ask him where he has been, who he has been with, and what he was doing. To ask those kinds of things is showing an interest in what is going on in that child's life. If they resent you asking those questions, they may very well have things going on that they do not want you to find out about.

The less a child has to hide the more accountable he will be willing to be.

I firmly believe that a parent needs to be involved in the activities of their children. If they are involved in sports at school then the parent should be at the games as much as possible to be supportive. How else will the parents be able to see how their child responds to different situations in life?

If schedules make it difficult to be as involved as you would like to be, then at least be involved as much as possible. Parenting is not just something that happens at home. Parents need to know what is happening in all the areas of their child's life. I doubt there is any acceptable excuse for a parent not being in fairly consistent communication with their child's teachers at school. Parents need to know what is happening with their child in school. Report cards are not enough. What possible reason could be good enough for a parent to avoid getting to know the people who probably spend more time with their child than they do?

Teachers have an incredible impact on a child's emotional, intellectual, and relationship growth. To let that all happen year after year without being involved is not good at all. That may be the easy way out, but it is poor parenting. To not know, and approve, what movies, music, and people your child spends his time with is taking a tremendous risk.

I have heard parents say that they trust their children so they do not pay attention to those things. That statement may sound noble but is asking for trouble. If children did not need specific input and help in making responsible decisions at different stages of their childhood, then there would be no need for parents or this book.

4. PERMITTING A CHILD TO DIVIDE AND CONQUER

Even in the most harmonious of families it is not unusual for parents to differ in their perceptions of what proper parenting means. They may agree on what is right and wrong behavior, but differ on how they should respond to them. Kids will learn very quickly what they can get away with around each parent. They will learn exactly what limits each parent has. They will know which parent is easier to manipulate.

I have asked many a child which one of his parents was the easiest to manipulate. They will usually get a big grin on their face and launch into an explanation of what vulnerabilities each parent has. They know exactly how to manipulate their parents to get what they want. They know just how long, or how hard, they have to push before they will get their own way. I have interrupted arguments before and asked them to predict the outcome of their argument. More often than not they both knew what the outcome would be. They just had to play out the scene to its inevitable conclusion. The parents are typically very frustrated about this because they know that ultimately they are not in control of the situation. They know that they have turned the control over to the child. They put up a token fight but ultimately submit to the predetermined conclusion of the child getting what he wants.

A particularly bad scenario is when the parents can be worked against each other. There is serious trouble when a child is told "No" by one parent so then he goes to the other parent to try for a different answer. The fact that the parents allow that to happen is no good. The fact that the child will use that to manipulate his parents to get what he wants should not be surprising. Do not ever let your child use divide and conquer tactics with you.

Children will also take advantage of parental conflicts that do not even directly involve them. They will know if you are especially vulnerable during a marital argument. They will know if you can be manipulated more easily when you are disciplining one of their siblings. They will know if that is the best time to put on their halos and approach you for something they would not normally approach you for.

5. BEING TOO QUICK TO ACCEPT EXCUSES

Most any child can become an expert at making excuses for not doing what they know they should do. If they can find someone who will accept their excuses as valid, there will be no end to their excuse making. Part of the problem is that many excuses can sound very convincing.
Sometimes the line between reality and the excuse can be very difficult to discern.

Take, for example, the child who is allowed to do poorly in school because someone has said he is hyperactive. The message there is that the child is totally helpless to adjust his behavior, and so cannot be expected to pay attention in school. Now, before you want to tar and feather me, and send me somewhere terrible, let me acknowledge that there are indeed children who need extra attention and care because of medically diagnosed hyperactive conditions, but even they can usually make adjustments that will help them function better. I have seen too many times where it is assumed that a child has no control over his behavior because he has a certain diagnosis, so the child is never even challenged to find ways to function better.

An overactive child needs to learn how to control himself, or the over-activity will control him. To simply accept that as an excuse for poor performance in school or home is to do that child a severe injustice. I have worked with many doctors, school psychologists, and counselors who agree with that statement.

There are articles in the newspapers every day telling of someone who has committed a terrible crime against society. The article will often go into a long discourse about their past life. They often seem to be building a case which will somehow justify the aberrant behavior. Their behavior is often excused on the grounds that they were abused as children, were products of a broken home, or some other such excuse. Those are all challenges to overcome, but do not have to be the automatic ticket to helplessness and victimhood that so many make it.

Anyone who has the ability to think rationally also has the ability to choose their responses to life. If we think we can justify inappropriate behaviors because of what someone else did to us earlier in life, then we set ourselves up to be permanent victims. A parent's response to their child's behavior and attitudes can help the child develop that awareness before he ends up suffering the consequences of poor choices.

6. PARENTS BLAMING THEMSELVES - GOING ON GUILT TRIPS

Most parents are doing as well as they know how with their children. A child will learn very quickly if he can put his parent on a guilt trip for parenting styles. Many parents are being blackmailed by their children. This happens when the child holds his parents responsible for his own inappropriate behaviors and attitudes. When the child wants to do something, he need only remind the parents how inadequate their parenting is. He has learned how to play on the sympathy of the parent to get his own way.

The temptation is to take the side of the children. They can be very good at convincing you that they are innocent victims of poor parenting. I fell into that trap several times when I first began counseling kids. It did not take me long to find out that I was not going to help anyone when I took sides. Parents in this situation need to realize that children make their own choices on how they respond to life.

Children need to be held accountable for the decisions they make. They need the privilege of experiencing the consequences of their decisions. Too many parents rescue their children from natural consequences because they blame themselves. "If I had only been a better parent, my little angel would not be in this trouble now." If that child has any concept of right and wrong at all then he is responsible for the decisions he makes.

So, with that in mind, how should a parent respond if he gets a call from the police in the middle of the night with the information that their child is in jail, and the bail is $1.00? What should the parent do? Most parents would rush to the jail and rescue their wayward child. That is definitely the wrong thing to do. It almost seems cruel, but the best thing to do is to let the child stay in the jail for at least long enough for it to be a significant learning experience for him. I understand the safety issues involved in that scenario, so cannot fault the parent for making sure their child is safe while in the jail setting.

Otherwise, it is counter-productive to rescue them from the natural consequences of their choices.

Try not to rescue a person from experiencing the consequences of his behavior. A child who is rescued from the consequences of his actions has no reason to change his behavior. You are not doing him a favor by rescuing him. He probably will not like you for it at the time. Hopefully he will understand, and maybe even thank you for it, later. Those times he is sitting in jail, or experiencing some other consequence, is when you will be most tempted to rescue him. The times you do not rescue him are the times he is most likely to accuse you of being a poor parent. Do not be manipulated by that, or you will likely find yourself in similar situations again and again.

There is a program called Tough Love that espouses this idea. I do not necessarily agree with all of the tenants of Tough Love but in general I think their concepts are very sound. There are differing degrees of Tough Love that can be very helpful depending on the circumstances, so you would do well to become familiar with the concept.

SUMMARY

So there you have some examples of negative parenting responses. It is very difficult to change horses in midstream, so to speak. If you find yourself in some of these examples, do not despair. It will not be easy to change, but the effort will be worthwhile in the long run. You cannot just wake up one morning and begin implementing changes. If you determine that you need to adjust a well-ingrained parenting response, it is best to sit down with your children first and explain to them what you have realized, and what you are going to do about it. Discuss it with them. Help them understand your thinking. Expect some disagreement, but be firm. Many long-standing power struggles can be resolved very easily when you decide to let the child experience the natural consequences of his choices. You no longer have to be "the heavy." You can merely remind him that he was aware of what the consequences would be when he chose that behavior, so when he did it anyway, he chose the consequence, not you.

CHAPTER TWELVE

PROBLEMATIC THINKING

In this chapter we will take a look at some thought processes that children (and other people) engage in that are totally self-defeating. You may find a frown coming to your face as you read the next few pages if the things I mention sound familiar. With each thing I mention I will also suggest some appropriate responses you might try. Here goes:

1. THE VICTIM STANCE

PROBLEM:

Using statements like "I could not help it. He started it." "He did not give me a chance." In general, an attempt to blame someone else for his behavior or attitude.

RESPONSE:

Accept no excuses. Bring the focus back on the individual. This is where most parents say something brilliant like "Well, if everyone else jumped off the top of the Empire State Building, would you do it too?" The analogy is at least as old as that famous building, but still very good. Someone else doing something is never a good enough reason for us doing it. We each make our own decisions, and must live with the results.

2. THE "I CAN'T" ATTITUDE

PROBLEM:

Lots of people get entirely too comfortable with the words "I can't." When most people say they cannot do something they really mean they are just refusing to try.

RESPONSE:

Realize that "I can't" usually means "I won't." Tell the person that you are very aware that his statement has very little to do with his ability to do something, and much more to do with his willingness to do it. If you too easily accept "I can't" from a child, you may be encouraging him to be a quitter. He will learn that things requiring an effort are best left undone. I have a sign hanging in my office that says: "The one who says something cannot be done is usually being passed by someone who is doing it."

3. LACK OF A CONCEPT OF INJURY TO OTHERS

PROBLEM:

Some people do not seem to think about how their behaviors and attitudes affect the people around them. They seem to be very insensitive to the feelings and emotions of others. They may even do things that they are very aware will be emotionally painful to other people, but that does not seem to matter. They are willing to fulfill their own wants at the expense of others.

RESPONSE:

Point out very specifically how their behavior is hurting other people. Help them develop the ability to put themselves in the other person's place. He needs to learn to identify the feelings the other person would have. Role playing can be very helpful here. You can play their part while they play the person who will be most affected by the behavior in question. This can be lots of fun for the family. You could also use an established game like "The Ungame" to help in this process.

4. LACK OF EFFORT

PROBLEM:

Some people are unwilling to do anything that they find boring or disagreeable. They will usually engage in lots of self-pity and look for excuses for not continuing the effort. A good example of this is when someone calls into work or school and makes an excuse of being sick or something else so he can get out of that effort for the day. In other cases they might do just enough to get by instead of giving it their best effort. I have been a teacher at both the high school and the college level. I wish I had a dollar for each time I suspected that a student was skipping school that day simply because they did not have their homework done, or did want to take a scheduled quiz or test.

RESPONSE:

Point out that the real issue is one of responsibility. Point out that he has plenty of energy to complete those things that he wants to do. It is also good if you can make sure there are some consequences for his lack of effort, and lying to cover it up. It is amazing how some kids experience a miraculous healing of their sickness when something comes along that they want to do.

5. REFUSING TO ACCEPT OBLIGATIONS

PROBLEM:

Here we are talking about the person who says he forgot to do something, or some other similar excuse. He really knew what he was suppose to do, but did not want to do it. If he has to choose between something he wants to do, and something he knows he should do, he will satisfy himself first.

He may have a terrible memory when it comes to doing his chores or his homework, but his memory is perfect when it comes time for his allowance. Now I know that there are times when it is very legitimate to say that you forgot to do something because that is exactly what happened. Aside from needing to develop a reminder system if that happens too frequently, the issue we are talking about here is when the excuses are used to avoid obligations.

RESPONSE:

Point out to the person that he has no problem remembering the things that are important to him. Ask him how he would feel if you suddenly began forgetting your obligations to feed him, give him his allowance, or other such things that he takes for granted. It is good to have consequences attached to his "forgetting."

6. HAVING AN ATTITUDE OF OWNERSHIP OF THINGS THAT ARE NOT HIS

PROBLEM:

Some people seem to have the presumptuous attitude that they can use or take anything they want for themselves. This includes the person who seems to feel like he owns your time and attention, and gets angry if he does not get it when he wants it. He will very blatantly use, borrow, or steal things that do not belong to him. He will not bother asking for permission. He will make demands of you as if he is asserting his rights to you. When you confront him about it he will likely try to make it look like your problem instead of his.

RESPONSE:

Have clear consequences in place for this kind of behavior. Correctly define "borrowing without permission" as "stealing" and respond accordingly. Such a disregard for other people's possessions can lead to much worse behavior later. Talk to the person about how he would feel if the tables were turned. You can be sure he would not like it much. Try to help him see how his behavior affects the other people. Hopefully he will care enough to be motivated by that.

7. HAVING NO CONCEPT OF TRUST

PROBLEM:

Some people seem to think that you owe them your trust. A problem exists when that person accuses you of not trusting him. The fact that you have many reasons for not trusting him does not seem to matter. He will make every effort to make it seem like your problem instead of his own. At this point they often try to turn the tables on you. He will typically raise his voice and glare at you while telling you he does not trust you either, or use the opposite tact of showing you his best whimpering, helpless, victim look. Either of those approaches is designed to put you on the defense. If you stop to defend your honor at that point, then he can successfully divert the discussion away from himself.

RESPONSE:

Realize that it is appropriate to not trust someone who has consistently shown himself to be untrustworthy. It does not make you a poor parent if you do not trust your own child, so do not fall for that. You do not owe anyone your automatic trust. There is nothing wrong with expecting someone to prove his trustworthiness, especially after he has done something that has been untrustworthy. Point out specific examples of why you do not feel like it would be wise to trust him at that point. Discuss the reality that trust must be earned. Never let his betrayal of your trust go unnoticed. Help him see ways he can earn back your trust in progressive increments. If he has betrayed your trust, then you can help develop a plan for him to earn it back.

This is best done by developing a program where he has to be consistent in small things first. As your trust is renewed with smaller things, it will be easier for you to begin trusting him again with the larger things.

8. UNREALISTIC EXPECTATIONS

PROBLEM:

You probably know someone who is almost convinced that he can walk on water. They seem to think the world revolves around them. If they think something should happen, then that is reason enough to expect it to happen. To them, thinking it so makes it so. Of course with this kind of thinking, they will constantly be setting themselves up for disappointment and conflict with others. They will expect other people to fall into line to accommodate their every wish and desire. If they do not, he will feel cheated. His expectations of what should happen are so egocentric that he fails to consider that other people might have some expectations that are different from his own.

RESPONSE:

Try to get him to be very specific about his expectations. It is especially important to teach him to plan ahead. For a while he will have to very deliberately and consciously choose to consider what other people's thoughts and expectations might be. Helping him discuss his hopes and dreams with you will give you a chance to help him see other options that he may be ignoring. Help him see the connection between his disappointment in people and his lack of consideration for them. If he can begin to own some responsibility for this process, it will help him establish some consistency in his life.

9. IMPULSIVENESS

PROBLEM:

Society puts a lot of different labels on behavior that is done without a proper thought process. Sometimes they will call it impulsive. Other times they will call it spontaneous. More often than not, however, we are simply talking about jumping into things without considering what is really happening, or what the options or consequences really are. These people will be quick to make assumptions, and then act on those assumptions, without considering consequences. They may spend large sums of money that they should really be spending on something else. They just do not pause long enough to consider that. They will often make decisions based only upon what feels good at the time. They will usually not bother getting the facts before making decisions. They will often make serious decisions on hearsay and opinion, instead of getting the facts. Their motto could well be "Do not confuse me with the facts." When something goes wrong, they are quick to blame someone, or something, else.

RESPONSE:

Point out how a simple consideration of available facts would have made a different decision very obviously better. Help him see what assumptions he made in the process, and how those assumptions were not helpful. Discuss the difference between being spontaneous and making irresponsible decisions based upon poor information.

Be careful to not end up being a victim of someone else's irresponsible decision-making process. They probably expect you to rescue them from the consequences of their poor choices. I have seen so many parents approach financial ruin as they literally paid for the poor choices their children had made. If they are irresponsible in their spending habits, it can be a good practice to have them sit down and list all of the things they have bought in the last year or so. Then have them put the price next to each thing. Then have them add up the prices of all the items they do not use very much anymore. That will often make quite an impact on them if they value their money. I like the sign that says something like, "Your Failure To Plan Does Not Constitute An Emergency For Me."

10. FALSE PRIDE

PROBLEM:

You know you are dealing with false pride when you have someone who refuses to compromise, even on little points. They will take a stand on something, and will not be budged by any amount of logic or truth. Their stand is often deliberately taken in direct opposition of conventional truth. They seem to believe that them taking that stand will be sufficient to change the minds of everyone else involved. It would not be unusual if that person did not even believe what he was saying. He is just taking a stand for the sake of taking a stand on something that he knows will create a controversy. He loves to draw people into arguments just for the sake of arguments. He will insist on his point of view to the exclusion of all others. He will continue to cling to his initial position even if someone happens to prove him wrong with undeniable facts. Again, his argument is not for the sake of exposing fact. It is for the sake of having an argument.

RESPONSE:

Talk to him sometime when he is not in one of his arguing moods. It sounds a little tacky but try to catch him sometime when he may be a little more vulnerable to the truth. To simply challenge him on his behavior will not be effective.

It is better to try a "back door" approach where you help him see the truth without making a fight out of it. Show him examples of how we all make mistakes and that it is important to learn from them. I do not suggest that this is an easy process, because it definitely is not. It is sad that many of these people have to end up looking very foolish before they are willing to see themselves as anything less than totally perfect.

11. FAILURE TO PLAN AHEAD OR TO THINK LONG RANGE

PROBLEM:

Too often people are so involved in their current life that they fail to consider how their current behavior and decisions may impact their future. These people will seldom consider the future unless it is to accomplish something illicit. They will often find themselves suffering consequences that could have easily been avoided if they only had planned ahead a little. This could be something as basic as getting in trouble in school for not getting homework done. They will say they had no time, and have all kinds of good sounding excuses, when the real truth is that they simply did not plan ahead. To them, any excuse is sufficient. They may explain being late for an important meeting by saying they had to take a shower. They could not take a shower earlier because they were playing ping-pong. It never occurred to them to stop playing ping-pong sooner.

It is amazing how many kids will use homework as an excuse for getting out of something they do not want to do. Homework sounds like a very noble reason for not doing something else. Most of the time, though, the homework excuse is just a cover for being irresponsible.

Sometimes, however, they may do the exact opposite. They may have such a strong fantasy about their future (usually totally unrealistic) that they do not consider the present. It is great to dream about future possibilities but that should not interfere with the person's ability to be responsible today. I remember the example of a kid who was to inherit a large sum of money when he turned twenty-one, so he saw no reason to work hard in school today. He was totally motivated by external things instead of having the character to make the most of what he had today.

RESPONSE:

Do some goal setting with the person. Find out what kinds of things he would like to accomplish in the near and distant future. Discuss the basic things that will need to be done in order to accomplish those goals. Point out how much he will be helping himself by thinking through the process.

Reinforce positive results that occur as a result of planning ahead. Those positive results could be something as simple as having a little extra play time, or saving enough money to get something he wants. Help him develop the habit of keeping a weekly calendar that he can update along the way in order to get everything done. Model this behavior by doing the same thing yourself. If he sees you getting more done, and staying calm as a result of your planning, he may eventually be motivated to do the same thing.

12. HAVING A POOR CONCEPT OF SUCCESS AND FAILURE

PROBLEM:

For this person, success is something that needs to be instantaneous. If he is not a success overnight he will see himself as a total failure, and be ready to quit. He will look with contempt on those people who work hard and long to achieve their goals. He will develop very grandiose goals, and expect them to happen almost magically, and with very little or no effort. They will be amazed, and feel betrayed and angry, when they are not promoted to Senior Vice-President two weeks after being hired as delivery boy. They will tend to see authority figures only as useful creatures available to elevate them to their rightful, lofty place in society. Anyone who is perceived as interfering with achieving their goals will be seen as the enemy.

They will also be very creative in their explanations of why they were not the instant success they told everyone they would be. Of course it will not be their own fault. It will be a boss, co-worker, or teacher who did not like them, or was unfair in some way. They will see themselves as victims of society instead of seeing the need to reevaluate their goal setting and achievement process. They will be a lot like the junior high boy who has a different girlfriend each week. Each girl will be "the one and only" for him.

They will have a new "goal of a lifetime" every week. Each new project will be the one that will catapult him into the *Who's Who of Business Successes*. Somehow, though, they just keep bouncing from one thing to the other. Each time they will be very surprised and upset that success was not thrust upon them immediately.

One of the dangers with these people is that at some point they may simply see themselves as total failures in life, and give up trying. If they cannot be at the top then they will often see the only option as being permanently at the bottom.

RESPONSE:

It may be helpful to take much the same response as we did with the person in #11 above. Get involved in the person's goal setting process, and help him map out a reasonable process for achieving that goal. If they will read, it can be very helpful to get them to read some biographies of people whose successes they respect. These biographies will usually point out the struggles, and even failures, the person had to go through on the way to his success.

Reinforce the idea that it is good to learn from our mistakes. Help the person see where he might have done some things differently to increase his chance for success.

13. FEAR OF BEING PUT DOWN

PROBLEM:

This is the person who cannot handle even the smallest criticism. This is true even if it is offered in a very sensitive way, and designed to be helpful. When even the smallest thing does not go his way, he will feel completely demoralized. He will struggle valiantly to place the blame for any negatives on other people. To suggest that he might have done something differently is to ask for an argument. This is especially tough when the person is also one of the people we mentioned that sets unrealistic goals for himself. He will set an unrealistic goal for himself, and then feel totally put down and defeated when he does not accomplish it quickly. He is less likely to attempt a new goal for quite awhile after his perceived failure. He will be too busy licking his wounds. He may even be a little paranoid about how other people perceive him and so may be defensive much of the time.

RESPONSE:

Point out how constructive criticism can be one of the best things that ever happen to a person. Help him differentiate between insults and criticism so he can try to glean positive from the criticisms. Discuss ways that he can adjust his thinking so his perception of criticism is not so negative. Maybe you can model how to decide which criticism has merit and how to ignore the rest. Point out the sense of personal satisfaction he can have when he stays in control of his emotions instead of getting all upset. Help him practice the process of critiquing his own actions and attitudes. Encourage him to make necessary changes before someone else feels the need to confront him about them.

14. REFUSAL TO ACKNOWLEDGE FEAR

PROBLEM:

There seems to be an unspoken law among many kids that they should never acknowledge fear. They may try to prove to each other how tough they are by denying fear of any kind. It is as if having a lack of fear is something noble. To acknowledge fear would be seen as weak. Since occasional fear is a very normal part of life, the child is then forced to hide his fear or be rejected by his peers. Of course we do not want our children to go to the extreme of having neurotic fears. It is just as bad, though, if they take this denial of fear to the other extreme. Their response to fear can go past a simple social response and become internalized to the point where the child totally denies the reality of those feelings. In order to maintain this facade, he is forced to suppress his feelings to the point where even he does not recognize them. Part of the danger of this is that those emotions will indeed be expressed at some point. When that happens, they will often be expressed in explosive, socially inappropriate ways. This, of course, can result in some very unhappy times for him and others around him.

RESPONSE:

At the very least it is important to talk to the child about the value of all emotions, including anger and fear. Point out that experiencing different emotions provides clues to us about how well we are functioning in situations. By appropriately responding to emotions instead of denying them, we can make positive adjustments that may end up reducing the negative impact of that situation.
To simply repress the emotion not only will not help, but in fact will just make things worse. Point out that it truly is a sign of strength to be able to face an emotion and deal with it openly and appropriately. To not deal with a situation will leave it to continue being a source of fear. To deal with it at least gives you the chance to remove it as a continuing source of negative.

Fear of receiving a speeding ticket motivates us to drive the speed limit. That simple adjustment of behavior totally removes a source of fear. Fear of failure keeps us motivated to do a good job. We then can enjoy the results of our efforts instead of dealing with another failure.

15. MANIPULATION THROUGH INAPPROPRIATE ANGER

PROBLEM:

We probably all know someone who is emotionally very intimidating. I am talking about the person who knows people will back down, and let him have his own way, if he raises his voice and projects anger at them. That anger may take the form of direct threats, intimidation, sarcasm, annoyance, or even assault.

I especially want you to notice that one of sarcasm. There are many people who seem to major in sarcasm. They do not openly demonstrate their anger, but instead express it through sarcasm. I know a lady who verbally cuts other people to shreds with a smile on her face. She would likely deny feeling anger. She often has to follow up her statements with telling her "victim" that she is only kidding. She has obviously grown very good at controlling other people with the anger she expresses through her sarcasm.

Parents have quite a challenge on their hands when their child learns to control through anger. Power struggles will become regular occurrences. It is even worse if the parent does the same thing. Volume levels will rise as they each try to out-intimidate the other one. Threats will be made. Ultimatums will be leveled against each other. Everyone will be frustrated. Nothing will be solved.

These kinds of inappropriate anger are really a sign of insecurity. They reveal a thought process of "might makes right." These kinds of anger will be like a tumor that will grow and spread until it kills a relationship.

RESPONSE:

Realize that most anger is a result of fear or insecurity. The person may be afraid that something will not turn out the way he wants. He may be afraid of being embarrassed or afraid of feeling helpless. He

112

may have learned to respond to those fears with anger. Anger is always a secondary emotion - that means there is always another emotion that comes first. Help him explore what the primary emotions are. In other words, what emotions came before the anger? Help him see that simply getting angry about something really is not productive in the long run. Discuss with him more appropriate ways of responding to those emotions. Help him evaluate his expectations of other people and situations to see where they might be unrealistic, and therefore leading to anger. Refuse to participate in any power struggles with him. Point out what is happening when you see it beginning. Purpose to model appropriate behavior by making your response a correct one.

SUMMARY

In this chapter we have discussed many of the things that literally keep a child from developing a positive emotional maturity. If these things are allowed to grow with the child, you can be sure that he will always be an unhappy person, and will probably contribute to the unhappiness of many other people as well. He may have periods of success and even happiness, but there will always be the underlying emptiness that comes with the things we discussed. If these things have already stabilized in your child, you may need the help of a professional counselor. Try the things suggested first, but get help if it does not work.

CHAPTER THIRTEEN

LEARNING A NEW LANGUAGE

Several years ago I accepted a very difficult challenge. I put myself in a position of needing to learn a new language. Since I was spending most of my time with people who only spoke Spanish, I found it necessary to learn that language myself. I could have probably survived without learning to speak much Spanish, but I knew life would be a lot easier if I could communicate with them in their own language. The same thing is true of you if you expect to be able to effectively communicate with your children, or anyone else for that matter. Even though they may use words that are familiar, they may be speaking an entirely different language. Many Spanish words sound very much like English words. I cannot respond to them according to what English word they sound like, though, because they often have a totally different meaning.

If you do not learn what the words mean in the language your kids use, you will very quickly lose much of your effectiveness as a parent, because you will not really understand what they are saying. You will likely end up very frustrated because your responses to their words will not be helpful.

In this chapter I am going to give you some examples of what I mean by that so do not despair. If you can learn to respond to what is meant, instead of to what is said, you will become much more effective in your efforts to discipline.

Having said all of that, here is a list of statements often made, and what the underlying meaning is really likely to be:

1. "I can't." means "I won't."

2. "I will try." means either:

    (a) "I will not." or

(b) "I will give it a little effort so you will get off my back, but do not expect me to succeed."

3. "Yes, but … "means "No." Or "I won't."

4. "I like to argue." means either:

(a) "I feel superior by putting others down." or
(b) "I feel a need to compete with people."

5. "I should…" means "I know what I should do, but I really do not want to do it."

6. "I am moody." means:

(a) "I can do anything I want, and so I will use my emotions to discourage you from trying to deal with me."

(b) "If I feel badly it is your fault." or
(c) "I will keep you guessing about my true feelings."

7. "I am stubborn." means "I am going to do what I want and I challenge the world to stop me."

8. "I am an individual." means "No one can make me do what I do not want to do."

9. "I am sensitive." means:

(a) "My feelings get hurt very easily."
(b) "If I cry or get hurt it is your fault, so just quit bugging me." or
(c) "I need you to constantly reassure me."

10. "I am timid or shy." means:

(a) "I force attention upon myself." or

(b) "I want you to prove to me that you want me around, so you have to beg me to be involved." (If he is at a party and everyone is dancing except him, whom do you suppose people will notice? Him, of course. Acting shy or timid can often be the most effective way to get noticed.)

11. "I worry a lot." means:

(a) "I control others by trying to make them feel guilty for causing me pain." or
(b) "I replace action with worry and therefore avoid having to resolve the problem."

12. "I feel guilty." means:

(a) "I will continue to do what is wrong." or
(b) "I have to convince the world that I have good intentions. I just have this one area of my life that I cannot control."

13. "It is a habit." means:

(a) "I am an innocent victim." or
(b) "I do not really plan to change so you might as well get used to it."

14. "I am confused." means "I do not want to make a decision so you might as well quit pressuring me."

15. "Be careful what you say." means:

(a) "I am angry."
(b) "You had better be careful because I will get even if I do not like what you say."
(c) "I am willing to threaten you if that is what it takes for me to stay in control."

16. "My children are not cooperative." means:

    (a) "Help! I am really frustrated, angry, and feel helpless."
    (b) "My children will not do what I ask them to do."

17. "I am only human." means:

    (a) "I really do not have very much respect for myself."
    (b) "I do not see much hope for me changing my life."

18. "I feel threatened." means:

    (a) "I feel like I am losing control."
    (b) "I am afraid."

19. "I am ambivalent about this." means:

    (a) "I am unwilling to take action to solve my problem."
    (b) "It is safer to not make a decision."
    (c) "I want it both ways so I do not want to make a choice."

20. "I cannot decide." means:

    (a) "I will not decide." or
    (b) "I am afraid to make a decision."

21. "I do not care." means "I really care very much but I do not want other people to know what I am feeling."

22. "I am not ready for..." means "I am not willing to..."

23. "You are my last hope." means "I have not let anyone else help me and I am not going to let you help me either. Feel free to knock yourself out trying though."

24. "I do not know." means:

(a) "I will not tell you."
(b) "I do not want to commit myself."
(c) "You tell me so I can blame you."

25. "I am lonely." means "I want someone to take care of me."

26. "I have no ambition." means:

(a) "I do not want to do it."
(b) "I am lazy."

27. "Who am I?" means "I am struggling to conform the world to my personal desires."

28. "I have a temper." means "I need to intimidate to get my way." (We do not lose our tempers. We use them.)

29. "I cannot forgive." means:

(a) "I am going to hold this deed against the other person."
(b) "I get a feeling of superiority or being in control when I do not forgive."
(c) "I can feel morally superior when I can convince myself that someone should not be forgiven." i.e. "I am too good to excuse that behavior."
(d) "My unforgiveness gives me an excuse to stay away from that person."

30. "I cannot keep friends." means:

(a) "I wish to dominate others."
(b) "I am not willing to be flexible with people."
(c) "I do not want to be sensitive to the thoughts and feelings of others."
(d) "If people do not cater to my wishes, I just reject them."

31. "I am a rebel." means:

(a) "I refuse to submit to life unless I get it my way."
(b) "I must be in control at all times."

32. "I am a procrastinator." means:

(a) "I really do not want to do that."
(b) "Look at how great I am when I get something done last second."
(c) "I am really too lazy to give that project my best effort."
(d) "I am too irresponsible to schedule my time appropriately."

33. "I am an alcoholic." means:

(a) "I control my world through my drinking."
(b) "I set up artificial supports to get me through life."
(c) "I am a victim."

34. "I daydream a lot." means:

(a) "I cannot get what I want out of reality."
(b) "I can have life on my own terms while I daydream."

35. "I am a joiner." means:

(a) "I am trying to find out where I really belong in life."
(b) "I must prove to myself and others that I am acceptable by becoming a part of every group of people possible."
(c) "I am afraid of being left alone with myself so I must be busy all the time."

36. "I am bored." means:

(a) "I am lazy."

(b) "I expect you to keep me sufficiently entertained. If you do not, then I will conclude that you are a poor parent, and blame you for my boredom."

And the age-old favorite...

37. "That's just the way I am." means:

(a) "I have already convinced myself that I am a victim, so do not try to take that away from me."
(b) "I need you to believe that I am helpless so you will either take care of me, or at least not expect me to change."
(c) "I am far too lazy to try to change."

I encourage you to use these things just as guidelines. Our minds tend to work in different ways at different times. The meaning of our words may also vary according to the circumstances. I think you will feel a lot better about your ability to communicate with people, though, when you become more aware of what the underlying message often is. There are times, of course, when the words mean exactly what they say. The goal here is to learn to recognize when these types of things are being said as a way to justify something negative.

CHAPTER FOURTEEN

AGE APPROPRIATE BEHAVIOR

In this chapter we are going to take a look at what behavior can be considered appropriate for various age groups. We will then look at some positive responses to those behaviors. Parents do a great injustice to their children when they expect them to obtain a level of behavior, or awareness, that they are simply not ready for yet. It is equally unjust to let a child get away with behaviors that he should have learned to change by now. Let's take a look at some of those behaviors.

6 - 7 YEARS OLD

BEHAVIORS:

Children in this age group are usually in a stage of strongly identifying with one of their parents. The "preferred parent" at this age is often the father. This can make it especially tough on the mother because the child may blame her for everything that goes wrong. The dad will often be seen as the hero that does nothing wrong. This child will be quick to tell all of his friends what is happening in your home. He will no doubt embellish his story so his situation seems better or worse than everyone else's. He is very invested in being a winner at this age. Consequently, he will likely be very rigid and demanding. He may develop a very negative attitude, and will get angry very easily, when anyone attempts to challenge or criticize him.

RESPONSE:

It is especially important for parents to be consistent with children in this age range. Since the child is trying to develop a sense of individuality, it is good to let him struggle through some decision-making processes. Be there to help him if he is willing to be helped.

Be careful, though, to not impose your "help" when he does not want it. Let him settle his own differences with people as much as possible. Realize, though, that adult supervision is necessary most of the time. Just do not be too controlling. Provide lots of opportunities for the child to play with other children of his age group. Try to avoid games that have a winner and a loser. Reinforce positive behaviors where possible. Talk with him about good decisions he has made, and help him see why they were good decisions. Let him experience the natural consequences of his decisions as long as they will not harm him. Help him understand that winning may not necessarily mean coming in first. Be sure to reinforce positives whenever possible.

7 - 8 YEARS OLD

BEHAVIORS:

This child will often seem to be very disagreeable. He may openly disagree with both of his parents. He will not have much of a middle ground when he talks about how he feels about someone else. He will either like them or hate them. In this disagreeable state of mind it should not be too surprising that he may get into verbal, and even physical, fights with his peers. He will not likely be a good loser. He may be aggressive, moody, and sulky. He may feel like no one likes him and everyone is against him. He will argue a lot and be very sensitive to criticism.

RESPONSE:

Try to be really patient with this child. Just because he has some bad attitudes right now does not mean he is destined for a reprobate life of crime. It just means he is really struggling with his perception of himself and his relationships. Show understanding and concern but be careful to not "smother" him. Let him have his say as often as possible and let him be "right" at times. That does not mean you have to sit back and condone rebellion by your silence. It just means to let him express himself where possible. Let him know that you value his input. Give him your undivided attention when he is trying to let you know what he thinks or feels. Try to respond to him in a way that does not set up a power struggle. If you just tell him he is wrong without following up on that, you will have done more harm than good. Developing positive communication with him now will pay a lifetime of dividends. Provide him opportunities for loosely organized games with his friends. Try to prevent problems from escalating very far, or you will have numerous fights on your hands. The danger is that the child will simply learn that the best way to solve problems is by force, and that might makes right. Adult supervision is highly recommended when several kids of this age get together to play. This is also the age when it is good to give the child opportunities to learn skills that he can develop a competency in. Examples of such skills would be swimming, ballet, softball or baseball, etc.

8 - 9 YEARS OLD

BEHAVIOR:

By now the child is trying to rely less and less on his family. He is likely to be more confident about expressing his opinions. Bickering will often become more common now. This can be a difficult time because he is becoming more sensitive to how other people perceive him. At this point he is even more critical of himself. He may withdraw at times and seem to be more secretive. He may seem to daydream more and have very little patience with things that do not go his way. His moods may change very rapidly. One minute he may be very pleasant, cheerful, and introspective, and the next minute he may be very angry, demanding, or rebellious. This age child also tends to only be interested in same sex activities such as Boy Scouts or Girl Scouts.

RESPONSE:

It is good at this age to encourage him to be involved in activities outside the home. It would be very positive to encourage him to be in Boy Scouts, or to play on a baseball or basketball team. Be willing to "go with the flow" of his moods. Try not to make a big deal out of a mood change. It will probably change again before you have finished anyway. Do not take things too personally if he wants to have some independence, or challenges what you say at times.   Give him a secure place where he can keep personal things without having to worry about other people intruding. Keep your sense of humor. It will help you when nothing else will.

9 - 10 YEARS OLD

BEHAVIOR:

At this age it is easy for the parent to get a false sense of security with the child. The child is likely to become much more affectionate with his parents. He may want to spend more time with the parent, and even openly try to imitate the parent. He may start being much more selective about whom he has as his friends. It is not unusual for children this age to find a "hero" he admires and try to pattern every part of his life after that person. Lots of parents panic when they see the "hero" their child picks, but try not to over react. At this age the child may seem much more relaxed and accepting of life. He will not seem to have many fears or concerns about what is happening in life.

RESPONSE:

This is a good time to let the child have a little more freedom in setting his own rules. Keeping the lines of communication open is especially important at this time, so try to spend lots of time in meaningful communication. Talk to him about his decisions. Talk to him about his friends. Let him talk about his heroes, and try not to be too critical of his hero if the person is someone you do not approve of much. This is a good time to talk about decision making, and to reinforce positive attitudes and behaviors as much as possible. The process here is actually one of building the best possible foundation with your child before he gets into his teenage years. The more quality time you can spend with your child now, the better it is going to be for both of you later on. I have also seen parents who become very jealous of the 'hero' their child is giving attention to, and have caused a lot of strife in the process. If you are one of those parents, please realize that the jealousy is just an expression of your own insecurity, and must be dealt with without imposing it on either the child or the 'hero.'

10 - 12 YEARS OLD

BEHAVIOR:

If we describe ages 9-10 as the quiet years, then I guess we need to describe ages 10-12 as the rebel years. At this age he will often resent being told what to do. He will rebel against routines and will strive for every bit of independence he can manage. He may be uncharacteristically quiet around strangers, but will be openly critical of adults he knows - this includes his parents. His mood swings will be frequent and extreme. As a parent, you may be tempted to lock your child up in a closet until he grows out of this stage. One good thing is that he is likely to enjoy participating in community activities that allow him to interact with peers.

RESPONSE:

During this time parents may develop a very sore tongue. I say that because you will definitely need to be biting yours to keep from saying some things that beg to be said. It is important to learn when not to talk. He will tend to just label you as a nag and ignore you if you complain too much, so try to control yourself. Give lots of approval whenever he does something positive. Give him independence and responsibility as he is able to handle it. There may be some fine lines when it comes to independence and responsibility. You do not want to give him too much, or too little, of either one. He will no doubt try to convince you that he can handle much more of both than is reasonable, so clearly define limits. It will be helpful if you can be involved in his decision making processes, but you have to do that very carefully or he will reject it. Help him set his own schedule within the limits that you allow. Be willing to be flexible. Give him an opportunity to prove himself if he disagrees with one of your limits that you can be flexible with. Part of the challenge here is that kids will often try to "grow up too fast." Parents sometimes really like that because it seems to take some of the pressure off them. Do not push your child too fast. Let him be a child until it is time for him to be an adult.

12 - 18 YEARS OLD

BEHAVIOR:

Welcome to the adolescent years! These years are definitely the wonderfully dreadful years. These kids will try your patience in every imaginable way. Sometimes you will not know whether to hug them or yell at them. These kids will test every imaginable limit and control that you or society tries to "inflict" upon them. They will want to be treated like a little child one minute and like a totally independent adult the next minute. They will systematically question, and seemingly reject, every parental value, idea, and preference you have ever tried to share with them. They will usually spend much more time with friends and so, consequently, much less time with the family. Family traditions will be challenged and anti-societal norms will be flaunted. They will explore this new area of sexual feelings and often haphazardly try to integrate those feelings into everyday life. School and home responsibilities will be seen as unnecessary interferences. The boyfriend/girlfriend thing may begin. Every girl or boy they "go with" will definitely be the one they have been looking for their whole life. "Lifetime" commitments will be made and broken with almost casual recklessness. They will likely have periods of time when they are very quiet, and then other times when they cannot be slowed down. At times they will seem to be hyper-responsible but as soon as you get excited about that it will be replaced with a "who cares" attitude. One day you will be so proud that they have become such fine human beings, and the next day you will be wondering what keeps them out of prison.

RESPONSE:

Somehow, as if by some kind of miracle, most of these kids become responsible, well-adjusted adults. You may find it impossible to picture that happening now, but hang in there. Try not to make a big deal out of behavior which is not that significant. Do not major on minors. By that I mean to try not to make a big deal out of little things. If you over-react with the little things then you will be totally helpless when something larger comes along.

I cannot overemphasize the importance of being a good model at this point. Give your best effort to set the example of being a respectful, polite, patient adult. Even though they may seem to be rebelling against you in every possible way, they will be watching your life very closely. They would deny it categorically, but most kids imitate many of their parents' behaviors and attitudes. If it is acceptable for you to do something then they will consider it acceptable for them also. Be honest about your thoughts and emotions, but be careful to express them in a way that respects your teenager's opinions and emotions. Model correct expression of anger and frustration. Point out the natural consequences that come along with the decisions they make. Allow him to experience those consequences as much as possible. Encourage and welcome your teenager to bring his friends into your home. Expect them to abide by the rules of the house, but try not to be too controlling. Your child wants to be able to be proud of you around his friends, so be extra careful how you treat him when his friends are around.

Communication technique is especially important at these ages. Now is when you will reap the benefits if you developed open communication with them during their earlier years. No topic should be off limits as long as it is discussed respectfully. Do not be afraid to discuss very personal issues like sexuality. If they know that you will respect their feelings and ideas then they are more likely to listen to yours. Be very open about potential positive and negative consequences of various types of sexual behavior. Do not wait for them to learn about it in school or from their friends. To do that is to ask for trouble. If you expect them to have a moral understanding of various sexual issues then you need to be willing to openly discuss it at home. Provide them good reading or other material on sexuality, body changes, etc. If you are uncomfortable with this, then get some training for yourself so that does not become a barrier between you and your child. Learn what words are being used to describe various behaviors and attitudes of the day. Every generation seems to have a set of words that are unique to them. If you do not learn those words, your ability to understand and communicate with them may be hindered.

Counsel, rather than judge, behaviors and attitudes. Your input will be quickly discounted and ignored if you have a judgmental or condemning attitude. This comes back to what I said about demonstrating caring and warmth in a non-threatening manner. This also reinforces the idea of modeling appropriate responses and ways of conveying affection. If you spend your time watching television shows or movies where inappropriate sexual attitudes and behaviors are involved, then do not bother trying to tell them something different. Your behavior will speak too loudly for them to hear your words.

Make sure your child has adequate privacy. He should be able to go into his bedroom, close the door, and not have to be concerned about someone coming in without his approval. It is normal for a teenager to want to spend significant amounts of time alone. Of course we do not want that to become extreme, but them spending time alone is usually nothing to be worried about.

There may be times during these years when you really do not feel like much of a part of your child's life. Try not to despair. If you have kept the communication channels open, those times will not likely last too long. Without being too pushy, you could help your teenager consider goals to pursue. Help him analyze and plan to accomplish those tasks. Challenge him to think through things when he gets too impulsive. Always highlight and compliment successes whenever possible.

CHAPTER FIFTEEN

DEFENSE MECHANISMS

In this chapter I would like to point out some behaviors called defense mechanisms. It is no secret that people do not like to experience emotional or physical pain. As we are growing up, we develop personalized ways to defend ourselves from having to acknowledge, or deal with, that pain. Those mechanisms that we use to defend ourselves against emotional pain or discomfort are called Defense Mechanisms. It is very important to remember that Defense Mechanisms happen at a subconscious level. They are not consciously chosen responses to emotional pain.

We all use defense mechanisms. I would even go so far as to suggest that we all need defense mechanisms. The problem comes when we abuse defense mechanisms. By abusing them I mean either using them too little or using them too much. Someone who does not have well-developed defense mechanisms will be at the mercy of every emotion he experiences. The person whose defense mechanisms are too strong will not have an accurate picture of what reality is in his life.

I am going to list and discuss several defense mechanisms here. As I do, you will no doubt see why this is such an important part of any discussion on discipline. If your child is subconsciously using defense mechanisms that keep him from accurately recognizing or facing reality, then it will interfere with your every discipline effort. Equally important would be the case where you may not see something even as clearly or accurately as your child because of the defense mechanisms in your own life. Let's discuss some of them and you will see what I mean.

1. DENIAL

Denial is the ability to subconsciously block out realities that people around you can clearly see. The teenager or adult with an alcohol or drug problem could be an excellent example of this. He will deny, and believe with all his heart, that he does not have a problem. He will very convincingly argue that he is in total control of his alcohol or drug use. He will make, and believe, statements like "I can stop any time I want to." He may even stop for a while to prove his point. Inevitably, though, the old behavior will return. People around him will be able to see that the problem is getting worse. He may be suffering social and physical consequences that everyone else knows are directly related to his alcohol and drug usage, but he does not see the connection. He will have an elaborate explanation of why that is happening that will not acknowledge the alcohol and drug problem. To try to get help for your child at this point will be very difficult because he will truly believe that you are wrong. He will be convinced that you are making a big deal out of nothing. This denial can be just as bad in lots of other areas of your child's life also. You may see that he has an attitude, behavior, or relationship that is destroying part of his life, but he will not see it at all. When you try to talk to him about it, he will accuse you of making it up or exaggerating. This will no doubt break your heart at the time because you both really believe what you are saying. Unfortunately this is a very difficult defense mechanism to break through. The Alcoholics Anonymous organization often talks about the need for a person to "hit bottom" before the denial can be broken. Hitting bottom is when the consequences of the behavior become so extreme that the connection between them and the behavior cannot be denied any longer. This process can often put everyone involved through a lot of emotional pain. Many families have been destroyed because of denial. If a person cannot accurately see how his attitudes or behaviors are affecting his or others' lives, then he will not be motivated to change them.

There is, however, a process called an "intervention" that has had considerable success helping people break through their denial. An intervention is when those people who are most familiar with, and most concerned about, the denied behaviors gather together at one time with the person. During that time together they very specifically discuss the behaviors they are concerned about. They give specific examples. They also let the person know exactly what their response will be if the behavior continues. They outline exactly how they hope the person will proceed to change that behavior. Many an alcoholic teenager and adult have received treatment as a result of an intervention. They were made to realize that their behavior would not be tolerated any longer. They were told that immediate treatment was the only acceptable response. Even if he continued to deny the drinking problem, he could not deny the current reality of what was happening in the intervention. These kinds of interventions are best done with the guidance of a professional who is familiar with how to make the intervention most likely to succeed.

2. RATIONALIZATION

The defense mechanism of rationalization can also be very frustrating. Rationalization is the process of explaining away inappropriate behaviors or attitudes with a bunch of inadequate excuses. Teenagers often become masters at this. They will come up with incredible excuses for their behaviors. Rationalization is difficult to argue with also because it usually sounds very logical. Remember that this is done subconsciously, and is totally believed by the person.

We are not talking about stretching the truth or lying here. Since we used the example of the alcoholic in the last defense mechanism, let's follow through with that. As you read this example notice how it all sounds very logical but ends up with the wrong result:

An alcoholic is scheduled to get off work at five o'clock in the afternoon. About four o'clock, though, he starts thinking about how terrible the traffic is that time of day. He has worked hard that day and so decides to reward himself by getting off work a little early to avoid the traffic. As he drives toward home he starts thinking about what his wife would say about him skipping out of work early. He figures she would not understand the traffic issue, so he decides to kill a little time so he would get home about the same time as if he got off work normally. He remembers that a friend of his usually frequents a local bar about this time so he will just stop by there to say hello. He also remembers that his wife gets upset if he stops to drink on the way home, so he promises himself he will only have one beer. Sure enough, his friend is there in the bar. He talks to his friend, has his one drink, and heads toward home again. Now wouldn't you know it, his friend had told him something that he decides another friend in another bar really needs to know, so he goes to that bar. On the way in the door he again promises himself to only have one beer. One beer later he is again headed home. At this point he thinks about how upset his wife is going to be when she smells the beer on his breath. He determines that she just will not understand the traffic problem and his need to talk to his friends. At that point he decides that if he is going to get yelled at he might as well make it worth, it so he stops in the next bar and drinks till late at night. He walks into his house at one o'clock in the morning. Sure enough he missed the traffic. And sure enough his wife is waiting for him at the door and is very angry. She confronts him but he is convinced that his behavior is justified. He is likely to say something like "I knew you wouldn't understand. I knew you would be like this, and that is why I drank so much. It is your fault I am home so late."

You may have been tempted to laugh as you read that story. Notice how each decision seemed to be made very logically. A story similar to that is lived out in many homes every day. Teenagers can come up with very "logical" reasons why they do what they do. They will be convinced that they have done the right thing. If the result comes out wrongly, then they will be able to explain why it is not their fault.

Your response to situations like this will have to be very specific. You will need to decide what the consequence will be if the behavior is repeated and then be sure to follow through with that consequence. It is not unlike the situation where a boss tells his employee that he will be out of a job if he is late for work one more time. To allow those behaviors to continue without appropriate consequences is not being helpful at all. Challenging defense mechanisms is seldom pleasant and almost always a very difficult process. To let your child's harmful defense mechanisms go unchallenged, though, is asking for the situation to become progressively worse.

3. PROJECTION

Many of these defense mechanisms are very similar in nature. You have actually already seen projection in action as you read about the last two defense mechanisms. Projection is the process of blaming other people or situations for what is going wrong in your life. This is when a person will subconsciously be convinced that he is innocent, and others are responsible for his problems.

In the defense mechanism of rationalization we pointed out where the husband projected the blame for his behavior onto his wife. He believed that he got drunk because his wife was unreasonable. Your children may believe they have no choice but to rebel against your authority. They may have convinced themselves that you simply do not understand them or are not being fair. Then they can go ahead with what they formerly considered wrong. Their consciences are clear because they are convinced it is not their fault. They may say they do poorly in school because their teachers are mean or pick on them. They may believe they lost the game because the referees were against their team. The policeman just "had it out" for them when they got ticketed for going 45 in a 25 miles per hour school zone. They "had to shoplift the candy" because you do not give them enough allowance. They "had to cheat" because the test was too difficult. I had one of my twelfth grade students complain very loudly once when I confronted him for cheating. He was indignant that I would confront him for cheating because I should have known that there was no other way to get good enough grades to get into college. The fact that he spends most of his time playing soccer and entertaining his girlfriend instead of studying didn't seem to enter his thinking. These are just some of many examples of projection -

blaming someone or something else for the consequences of your behavior.

Be careful you do not get drawn into arguments about who is right and who is wrong. Do not fall for it when they try to make you feel guilty so they can excuse their own behavior. Outline responsibilities clearly, and then be consistent with your expectations of them.

4. DISPLACEMENT

The defense mechanism of displacement might also be called the "kick the dog" syndrome. This is when we displace our responses to our emotions onto people or objects other than the one we are really upset with. Consider this example:

Your child has had a rough day at school. His teacher sent him to the principal's office for misbehaving. The principal gave him a note to give to you when he gets home. The child is really angry because he does not think it is fair. He cannot take his anger out on the teacher or principal so he takes it out on everyone else. He screams at people on the bus, kicks the dog when he gets to the yard, and slams the door when he comes into the house. When you ask him what is wrong he will probably yell "nothing" and storm to his room, again slamming the door as he throws his books on the floor. This is a good example of displacement. Everyone and everything within reach is likely to experience his anger. He is not in the mood to look at how his behavior and attitude led to him being sent to the principal's office. He only knows that everyone is against him, and no one is going to convince him otherwise.

You cannot tell people to not be angry, or to not have other emotions. Emotions are not that logical. If they were, we could just tell the kid to go stand in the corner until he was happy. Of course that does not work. What we can do, though, is put limits on what behaviors are acceptable when someone is feeling anger or some other emotion. We can make it clear that it is unacceptable behavior to kick the dog, or slam the door, when they are angry. We can attach other reasonable consequences to those behaviors so there is motivation to not do them. We can reinforce positive behavior. Realizing that these are subconscious thinking processes, we can discuss the process with them when they cool down. You have won a great victory if you can help the person bring his subconscious thinking into his conscious thought processes, where logic and understanding have a better chance of prevailing.

5. INAPPROPRIATE LAUGHTER

This may not seem to fit in really well with the other defense mechanisms we have discussed, but it is just as important. Many people cover up their emotional pain with laughter. I can look at my own life to see how I used laughter as a defense mechanism as a child. I was the "class clown" in school. I would crack silly "jokes" and do all sorts of strange things to try to get people to laugh. I can see now that I was really trying to get people to respond to me in a positive way. I needed their acceptance, and was willing to pay the price for it. I had a great deal of inner emotional pain but I was very fearful of letting people see that. My response was to try to cover the pain up with the opposite emotion of happiness. It really did not work. I had no problem making people laugh. I can remember people saying things like they knew they could always count on me for a good laugh. It felt good to hear people say that because that gave me at least a small sense of being wanted, or having value. It did nothing to take away the real pain that was being hidden inside though. My laughter was nothing more than a mechanism to defend myself against that pain. Many kids and adults are the same way. They use laughter to hide their real feelings. I once saw a lady laugh during the funeral of someone who had been very special to her. It was so obvious that there was no real laughter in her heart that day. It was just a cover for her pain. Watch people who are nervous and you will often see them defending with laughter. We even accept that being called "nervous laughter."

If you see your child, or someone else, using the defense mechanism of laughter, you can talk to them. Let them know that you sense other feelings behind the laughter. Let them know that you care, and would like to be the kind of friend to them that they can trust their true feelings with. It is a fortunate child who can come home to a parent they feel they can share their true feelings with.

6. PASSIVE AGGRESSIVENESS

Some people actually believe that they can hide their anger. I strongly suspect otherwise. They may have some success at it for a while, but before long the anger will start showing in other areas of the person's life. Passive aggressiveness is when you subconsciously express the anger or resentment you have toward a person, or situation, in indirect ways. This is most likely to happen when you do not feel free to express your feelings toward the person in more direct ways. Your child may not tell you he is angry with you. He may even deny it if asked. You can be sure, though, that he will find other ways to tell you. He may fail to complete a task in the desired fashion. He may go slowly when he knows you have a very important appointment to go to. He may develop a sarcastic attitude for no apparent reason. He may start telling inappropriate "jokes" where people or things similar to what his anger is directed toward are the victims, or made to look foolish.

Sometimes it is difficult to tell whether this kind of behavior is truly a subconscious defense mechanism or a carefully chosen "safe" way to express anger. Either way it can be best handled by discussing it with him. Let him know what you are seeing, and what you suspect is happening. If it truly has been subconscious behavior then bringing it to a conscious level should be helpful. If it was conscious behavior then discussing it will deflate its power.

7. REACTION-FORMATION

Reaction-formation is a defense mechanism that can best be described as over-compensation. You may recall the Atlas Body Building cartoon advertisements in various magazines. The first block of the cartoon would show this skinny, weak boy lying on the beach. In the background you could see this popular, muscular guy being admired by the best looking girls on the beach. In the next block the muscular guy was kicking sand in the skinny boy's face while the girls laughed. The thought box above his head revealed that he was making a commitment to himself to become so strong that he would be able to easily conquer the other guy, and take the girls away for himself. Of course the last frame would show him, now very muscular as a result of using the Atlas Body Building Program, kicking sand in the other guy's face while the girls swarmed to his side. That would be a good example of reaction-formation. The skinny guy went from one extreme to the other and neither one was really positive. He did what he did for all the wrong reasons and over-compensated in the process. Kids and adults alike can fall into the same kind of trap.

Reaction-formation is usually defending against intense feelings of inferiority. When you see this happening to your child, it is good to help him redefine how his self-worth is measured. If he sees himself as a failure then help him see where he is not. Help him see that all the external efforts will not change who he really is as a person.

8. WITHDRAWING

The defense mechanism of withdrawing is exactly what it says. The person withdraws from people or situations. This can be an actual physical withdrawing or an emotional withdrawing. The physical withdrawing is obvious. Some children may withdraw into their rooms and stay there for hours and hours.

I am not talking about when they have a project they are investing time into. I am talking about when they just go somewhere to be away from other people. They are literally hiding from life. Emotional withdrawing can be less obvious. Some kids and adults watch television so much because it helps them avoid facing other people or situations that they perceive as emotionally painful or scary. They may start reading books as a way of avoiding other things.

I counseled one kid who rode his bicycle 15 miles every day. His parents thought he was demonstrating a great motivation and dedication, and reinforced him for it. I assumed he did it because he enjoyed it, and even commended him for it at first. Later on I discovered he really did not enjoy it at all. It turns out that he rode his bicycle during a daily time when tensions tended to be highest at home. He quickly curtailed his bicycle riding when tensions at home were reduced.

Another example of withdrawing could be the man who puts in a great deal of overtime at his job. He may be reinforced for being such a dedicated worker when he is really just withdrawing from his family. If you suspect that your child, or someone else, is withdrawing, it is a good idea to try to talk to him about it. Tell him what your concerns are and let him know you care. See if you can identify what feelings underlie the behavior. Then you can talk about them and help the child find a more appropriate way to deal with them.

9. PSYCHOSOMATIC ILLNESSES

I mentioned earlier that you can only hold feelings in for so long. After awhile, they will start "leaking out" around the edges. I could use the example of a pressure cooker. You can put the cover on really tightly and turn up the heat. For a while nothing will seem to happen. After awhile, though, you need to release the pressure valve on top or you will have an explosion. People are much the same way. You can suppress emotions like anger, resentment, and fear for a while. You may smile and look like everything is going fine on the outside, but inside there is a pending explosion. Our bodies have a way of turning our emotional or psychological pressures into physical problems.

In other words, your emotions can make you sick if you do not handle them properly. Some of the typical physical responses might take the form of:

-frequent headaches	-lower back pain
-difficulty falling asleep	-asthma
-high blood pressure	-nightmares
-heart problems	-stomach ulcers
-grinding your teeth	-difficulty concentrating
-menstrual problems	-sore or stiff muscles

-waking up in the middle of the night & not being able to get back to sleep

Do any of those sound familiar? Now be careful to not over react here. Remember that we are talking about defense mechanisms. Just because someone is experiencing one or more of the symptoms listed does not automatically mean he is an emotional explosion waiting to happen. If someone is suppressing his feelings, though, it can be very helpful to know how the feelings might be getting expressed in physical ways. It gives you something to check when you start seeing them becoming a part of someone's life.

10. OBSESSIVE-COMPULSIVE BEHAVIORS

The last defense mechanism we will cover here is obsessive-compulsive behaviors. This is when a person subconsciously tries to suppress, or prevent, experiencing an emotion or thought by replacing it with another set of behaviors that become obsessive or compulsive in nature.

Being obsessive has to do with recurrent thoughts while compulsiveness has to do with repetitive behaviors. Let's take the example of the child or adult who becomes obsessed with concern about being dirty so engages in the compulsive behavior of washing his hands excessively. He may wash his hand a hundred times a day even though he is doing nothing so dirty as to require such activity. Consider the lady that washes the ashtray 25 times during your visit even though neither of you smokes. These kinds of behaviors are usually communicating that person's need for some kind of activity to help him defend against certain feelings or thoughts. If your child engages in such activities, it is best to have him seen by your physician as soon as possible.

SUMMARY

There are actually many more defense mechanisms that we could talk about here but I think we have covered some of the most prevalent ones. I felt like this was an important topic to cover because it is so easy for parents to respond to the behavior instead of responding to the emotions that may underlie those behaviors. You might get some temporary relief from certain behaviors simply by insisting they change. In the long run, though, nothing is helped that way. The best way to make lasting changes in these defense mechanisms is two-fold:

1. Help the person develop a conscious awareness of what has previously been subconscious. That will hopefully open the channels of discussion.

2. Determine what emotions or thoughts the mechanisms are defending against, and help the person develop constructive ways to deal with them.

CHAPTER SIXTEEN

CHILD ABUSE

I think that a book about discipline ought to spend some time talking about child abuse. This is a scary topic to many people. It tends to be one of those topics that many parents want to know more about, but are afraid to ask. There seems to be such a hysteria about this topic at times that parents may be afraid to bring it up in conversation for fear they will be suspected. I have known several parents who refused to call an agency about parenting classes because the name of the agency included the words "child abuse." Maybe if we talk a little about what child abuse is, and what it is not, it will help alleviate some of those fears.

It is probably a safe statement to say that abusive parenting is a learned behavior. That learning likely took place while they themselves were children. Most statistics show that a high percentage of abusive parents were also abused children. They grew up knowing only that abuse was part of how they were parented. Even though they may have made solemn, and vehement, resolutions to not treat their own children that way, the cycle continues. If they were raised in abusive homes, it is probably safe to say that many of their emotional needs were not met in appropriate ways. They probably suffer from a very poor self-concept, which is reflected in their entire approach to life. Since they grew up in a dysfunctional family themselves, they never had the opportunity to learn appropriate ways to express such feelings as anger, frustration, and helplessness. Since those are the exact feelings that an abusive parent is most likely to experience on a regular basis, it should not be too surprising that they respond to them poorly. When they are finally old enough to leave home, they do so with all of those emotional problems intact. The likelihood of those emotions then being inappropriately vented upon their own children is naturally very high.

Because of their poor personal family history, the abusive parent is not likely to have a very clear, or realistic, understanding of what kinds of behaviors can be expected from their children. They may be less likely to overreact to certain behaviors if they had a better understanding of what behaviors and attitudes are "normal" and which ones are not. Abusive parents often seem to expect a level of perfection in their children's behavior that is totally unrealistic. The parent may take it as a personal rejection if their child does not perfectly obey their every order. They may perceive every misbehavior as a rebellious power struggle that needs to be squelched. Since their perception of the behavior of their children is extreme, their response to those behaviors may also be extreme.

It is also fairly well documented that a person growing up in a dysfunctional family is very likely to marry someone from the same type of background. Of course this just tends to compound the problem. Now you have two insecure people who do not know how to correctly identify and respond to their emotions, while trying to raise a child that calls for great emotional strength at times. Their inability to look to each other for understanding and support just tends to escalate the problem. Parents in this situation may become "co-conspirators" in an effort to hide the results of their abuse from society. When abuse takes place, they will often lie for each other to keep others from discovering the truth. They live in constant fear of being discovered, which just serves to raise their level of stress even more. It is sad that often something really terrible has to happen before their behavior is discovered by people who can do something about it.

CHILD ABUSE DEFINED

Child abuse could be defined as inflicting unnecessary emotional or physical pain upon a child. This can occur at both ends of a spectrum. Some children's basic emotional or physical needs are so neglected that it can be constituted as child abuse. You hear stories occasionally of a child that was locked in his room for extended periods of time. That might be the extreme, but many children may experience the same thing to varying degrees that still constitute child abuse. Some children are fed so irregularly, or so poorly, that their health is threatened. The other end of the spectrum is when parents use extreme levels of force in their attempts to discipline their child. Without outside intervention by the proper people, the abuse will not likely stop on its own.

The abusing parent will often inflict the abuse during an emotionally charged moment that may only last a few seconds. During that short period of time, though, great harm can be done. The parent will often feel terrible about the abuse when it is over. Promises may be made that it will never happen again. The fact that the same promise has been made, and broken, many times before does not seem to matter. Stories will be concocted to explain the bruises or injuries. Some children live their entire childhoods with those kinds of episodes occurring on a regular basis. Some children never live to be adults because the abuse became too extreme once, or something accidentally happened while the child was being abused.

Any discussion about abuse must also include the issue of sexual abuse. Sexual abuse may not be seen as much of a discipline issue but I think must still be included in any discussion of child abuse. It is usual for a child who has been, or is being, sexually abused to not share that information with anyone else. The sexually abused child's emotions are far more likely to be expressed through other behaviors and attitudes. This again reveals the importance of trying to be aware of what is going on in a child's life as you make attempts to discipline. The child must always be held accountable for his behaviors and attitudes. If you just discipline behavior, though, without helping the child understand and adjust the relationship between his behavior and his life experiences, then you miss a tremendous opportunity to help the child. Just adjusting his behavior is not going to be that helpful to him if he still has to go back home to be subjected to further abuse. I will not try to go into the myriad of issues relating to sexual abuse, but you would do well to find a good book or class to become educated about this tragedy. I will include some suggested readings at the end of this book.

SOFT ABUSE

Let me discuss something I call soft abuse. You may not hear anyone else call this abuse and it will not likely be reported to the officials. I believe, though, that soft abuse does just as much harm to the child as almost any other kind of abuse. I am talking about the abuse you inflict when you degrade your child by calling him demeaning names like "worthless" or "failure." I am talking about when you reinforce a poor self-esteem by telling him he will never amount to anything or that you are sorry you ever had him. I have known more than one adoptive parent tell their adopted child that they wish they had never adopted him. By soft abuse I also include such things as letting your child spend hour after hour in front of the television watching demoralizing shows, or playing video games, because you are not willing to make the effort to really build a meaningful relationship with him. I am not talking about him watching some television or playing some video games. I am talking about when you allow that to be so much of his life that other areas are sacrificed. Like I said, you will not hear much about these kinds of things in most discussions about child abuse. I feel strongly enough about them, though, that I feel they should be included.

WHAT CHILD ABUSE IS NOT

So much discussion about child abuse has to be handled very carefully because there is often such a fine line between what abuse is and what it is not. Most of the time it is simply a matter of degree. Spanking is not abuse unless it is done too extreme. The definition of "extreme" is left to the person considering the situation. Isolated moments of yelling and screaming are not likely abusive but when it becomes the norm then it might be. When that line is crossed can be very subjective. Leaving a child alone sometimes may be just fine until it becomes extreme. Again the definition of extreme is up for grabs. It is very difficult to determine an operationally objective definition of child abuse. It can be so much in the eyes of the beholder. Some ridiculous court cases have been prosecuted when the

145

child cried "abuse" when his parent did nothing more than give the child a mild spanking. Even the child agreed the spanking was mild and yet the parents were still convicted of child abuse, and the child taken away from them. Other cases have presented undeniable proof that a child had been physically tortured and yet the parents were acquitted and the child sent back home. In several of those cases the child was later killed by the parent during another child abuse episode. I believe that both of those verdicts were ridiculous and in both cases the child was done a severe injustice by the court system.

INTENT

Child abuse does not necessarily require intent to harm. Many parents will tearfully admit to abusing their child even against their own desires and efforts. They just "lose control" sometimes and end up abusing their child. I am sure there are examples also of parents who have used more force on their child than they intended, and maybe even left a bruise, but cannot be accused of child abuse. On very isolated occasions I suppose most parents "lose their cool" and apply more pressure to a spanking than they intended. When they are aware that this has happened they will take steps to make sure it does not happen again. They will be more careful to not spank when they are angry or frustrated. They will find a different way to discipline. They will let the other parent do the spanking for a while. In short, they will identify and solve the problem. In those kinds of cases I do not believe that such an isolated incident can be classified as child abuse. It does not excuse the behavior. It just does not call for outside intervention.

There are a lot of good parenting classes available that can help you if you are concerned about the possibility of abusing your children. Many of these classes are available for very little or no cost, and virtually any day or time, so there is really no excuse good enough to not get help.

CHAPTER SEVENTEEN

ALLOWANCES AND BUYING THINGS FOR YOUR CHILDREN

My views on this topic usually do not get very high marks from the kids. This is especially true if the kids are accustomed to getting very high allowances.

PURPOSE OF ALLOWANCES

An allowance should not be represented as pay. The children are not being reimbursed for being faithful members of the family. I think it is very sad that kids often think that their parents owe them an allowance. That kind of thinking quickly reveals that something is wrong. I suggest that an allowance have two distinct parts:

1) A stable, nonnegotiable amount that is the same every week regardless of what attitudes or behaviors the child is exhibiting.

   This part of the allowance should be designated for such things as his school lunch, locker dues, and other such expenses that he normally has. At this point we are not talking about expenses for things he would like to have. We are talking about things that he is required to have. Since those are typical parenting expenses anyway, they should naturally be covered by his allowance. I am a big believer that as soon as the child is able to handle the responsibility, this part of his allowance should be given to him in lump sum at the beginning of each week. It then becomes his responsibility to spend the money wisely throughout the week. To give him his lunch money every morning before he goes to school is to rob him of a growth experience. He will benefit greatly from learning to budget his money to cover the expenses he knows he will have that week. As a parent, you have to resist the urge to cover his deficits when he impulsively spends his money on something other than for what it was intended. If you rescue him from his poor fiscal planning now, you can be sure that he will be back many more times for the same reason. Of course it is not necessary to make this part of the allowance match his expenses penny for penny. It is not a bad idea to "pad the account" a little so he has some flexibility. That brings us to part two of the allowance.

2) The second part of the allowance is what I call "the benefit package."

This part can be negotiable. Since the other part of the allowance is to cover predictable expenses, this part of the allowance is designed to "pad the account" a little so he has some flexibility in how he spends his money. This is where many parents go astray, though. They pad the allowance too much. You may think you are doing him a favor by doing that, but you are not. The less he has to carefully consider how he spends his money, the less good you are doing him. Young children may not have as much need for extra money, but it is still good to give them a little benefit package also. As children get older, their options for ways to spend extra money multiply rapidly. This is especially true when they start dating, or driving a car.

Now comes the tricky part. I said that part one of the allowance should be given under any circumstance. Part two, though, can be tied to that child's behavior and attitudes. I do not think a child should be paid to clean his room, wash the dishes, take out the trash, or other things that he should do simply because he is part of the family. I do, however, think he should be penalized if he does not do those things as expected. The second part of the allowance can be used in that process. At the beginning of the week the child should be able to count on receiving both parts of his allowance as long as he has met the expectations his family has of him. The idea is not one of rewarding him for being a good family member. Just being part of the family should be adequate to meet that need. The purpose of an allowance is to enable the child to meet his expenses and to have a little money left over to use as he pleases. An allowance is given to help the child learn how to budget his spending and to learn how to make responsible financial decisions. If his attitudes and behaviors in the family are not acceptable, then his "benefit package" suffers. Since part two is a benefit, then the benefit can be tied to his participation in what he is receiving the benefit from. I hope that is not too confusing. Let me try to put it another way:

The child is receiving a weekly financial benefit as a result of his being a part of his family. This benefit can be used as he sees fit. If he chooses to not participate in his family in a positive way, then his benefit for being part of that family is adjusted accordingly. That way he is not being paid to be a positive part of the family, but he is penalized for negative behavior.

As I mentioned elsewhere in this book, the penalties for inappropriate behavior should be predictable. Some families even make charts of what the penalties will be for not fulfilling a family obligation. The chart might reflect a $1.00 reduction in the benefit package if the garbage is not taken out as expected. These penalty amounts are best determined during a family meeting so everyone can be involved in the process.

The child should be expected to buy things like birthday cards, football game tickets, extra snacks, and other such things from his "part 2" money. Special expenses that he can plan ahead for should also be included so he has to learn to plan ahead with his savings. It can be a really good move to require each child to put a certain percentage of all money he receives from you in the bank. Some parents who do this require their child to have their permission to spend the bank money. That may not be a bad idea.

So what do you do when "surprise" expenses come, as they seem to do all too often? There is nothing wrong with helping your child meet those kinds of expenses. Remember our purpose here. The purpose is not to be a tightwad with the purse strings. The idea is to train your child how to be responsible with money. A child should learn that his financial condition will very likely be closely related to the way he manages his life. We could all tell stories of how very responsible people were in terrible financial shape because of situations beyond their control, so we must acknowledge that reality.

We could probably also tell of very irresponsible people who do not know what to do with all of their money. That does not in any way change the premise of what we are talking about here. To indiscriminately give money to your child is to do him a great injustice. Remember that this whole book is stressing the need to help your child develop discipline in his life. Financial discipline is at least as important as any other kind of discipline mentioned here.

This brings up another thought too. Brace yourselves kids - you won't like this part at all. I really believe that parents are very unfair to their children when they buy them a beautiful new car when they turn sixteen. We all know that every kid fantasizes of the day he can go get his license and drive off into the sunset in the car of his dreams. Why cheapen his appreciation of that experience by just handing it over to him? That may give him some temporary joy. He will no doubt smother you with "appreciation" at the time. For at least a little while he will be the happiest kid in existence. The fact that you spent a lot of money on the car, though, will not heighten his appreciation of it for long. Anything after that will be anticlimactic. What do you do for his graduation - buy him an airplane?

There is a real danger of teaching your child to be too materialistic. It is great for them to have nice things until they start to think you owe it to them. It is a proven fact that people will appreciate something more if they have a financial investment in it. At the very least have the child pay half of the cost of the car. He will treat it much better if he has to pay for at least half of the maintenance, gasoline, and insurance costs also. That may sound like a lot to expect from a kid, and it is. It is a lot for a kid to expect to have a car also. You can go out on the "main drag" any Friday night and almost pick out the kids

150

who were given their cars, and which ones had to at least help pay for theirs. There is usually a very qualitative difference in how they treat their cars. It is a whole lot better for your child to be proud of a modest car he helped get himself than to not be able to have that kind of pride with a car someone else gave to him.

Well, that may seem to be a lot of to do about nothing, but I think the point had to be made. Do not give your children everything on a silver platter. Let them have some personal pride by helping to earn what it takes to get those possessions. He may complain that "everyone else has one" or "my friend's parents bought him his." Those kinds of statements just support this whole argument. "Everyone else having one" or "everyone else is doing it" are not good enough reasons for him to have it or do it.

CHAPTER EIGHTEEN

SPARE THE ROD?

There are few topics as controversial as spanking. I do not want to add to a controversy but I would like to make some suggestions and encouragements about the subject. I am convinced that spanking is a positive parenting response to inappropriate behavior as long as it is administered with the correct understanding of its purpose.

Spanking is generally only effective with younger children. If they are too young to be able to relate to an intellectual discussion about something, then spanking may be very helpful. If the child is reaching for something that is dangerous and will not respond to a "No," then spanking is called for.

Spanking serves not so much as a punishment as a reinforcement that there are things that absolutely must not be done. Spanking provides an immediate way to reinforce a "No" statement. The parent should always be sure that the child is associating the spanking with the wrong behavior. Excuse the comparison, but it is much like training a dog. I see people sticking a dog's nose in a puddle he made on the floor ten minutes after the puddle was made. At the same time they are spanking the dog and yelling at him as if to make him feel guilty. The dog is not learning to go outside to make his puddle. He is learning that the puddle is bad. The same idea is true with little children who do not understand what you are saying very well yet. If you are going to say something, be sure to say it as the behavior is taking place, so the correct association is made. The same is true with spankings. Only delay a spanking if the person can fully understand why he is being spanked later.

Let me give an example of when a spanking would be appropriate:

A two-year-old makes a request of you that you decide should not be granted because it is time to go to bed. You respond by saying "No. You may not. It is time to go to bed now." The child gets angry and says "No. I do not want to go to bed" and starts to throw a tantrum. You say something like "Well, it is your bed time so you need go to your room now and put your pajamas on." He responds by saying no again and kicks you. I believe in letting a child express his emotions, but he needs to do that verbally and appropriately. Kicking is not appropriate. At that point a spanking is a proper response. To argue with him at that point is to teach the child how to have a power struggle with you. You need to extinguish that behavior before it ever gets started. Remember that "No." is a complete sentence. The child needs to learn as soon as possible that arguing with you will not be a pleasant experience for him. He needs to know that arguing, or throwing a temper tantrum, will not be helpful to his cause. The first day you let him have his way because he out-argued you will be the first day of a long power struggle between the two of you. Spanking is probably the most effective way to teach him that truth before he gets better with the other options. Never abuse your child, but spank him hard enough that it is an unpleasant enough experience for him to be motivated to not repeat the behavior. He needs to know that when it comes down to a matter of your will versus his will, that your will is to be followed.

Remember that spanking is not intended to be a punishment. It may sound like a word game, but spanking is intended to steer a child away from wrong or dangerous behavior. If a child is reaching for the light socket and will not listen to your direction, then you need to steer him away from that in a way that is meaningful to him.

There are some disadvantages to spanking also. That does not mean you should not spank, it just means to be aware of the disadvantages so you can respond to them properly. Here are a few of the disadvantages of spanking and suggested responses:

1) One of the main disadvantages is that spanking potentially teaches the child what not to do but does not teach him what to do. You can handle this by trying to reinforce the positive behavior that you would like to have replace the other

153

negative behavior. Do this as soon after the spanking as possible.

2) Spanking may also lead to frustration in the child because the spanking definitely represents a defeat for the child at the time. Some of our best learning opportunities occur during our times of defeat though. Sheltering your child from experiencing those defeats will not be helping him. Communicate as well as you can with the child so he can understand the point you are trying to make. We always hate it when someone says something like "You will thank me for this some day" but that is quite often the truth.

3) Children often imitate their parents so they may begin hitting other people. This again emphasizes the need to make the spanking clearly associated with their wrong behavior and not just something one person does to another person when they are upset.

As a child gets older, you should be able to replace spanking with the other discipline techniques outlined next in this chapter. You should have other techniques in place long before you find yourself saying something like "My child is getting too big to spank."

4) You want to avoid the thinking that "might makes right." Spanking is not intended to be a physical confrontation between two people. It is a unilateral response to an inappropriate or dangerous behavior. Some people complain that spanking just teaches the child to be violent. If that is what the child is learning, then the spanking is not being administered appropriately.

ALTERNATIVES TO SPANKING

There are some other responses that can sometimes be used successfully in place of spanking. Here are some suggestions:

1. You could eliminate the positive response the child expects to receive as a result of his behavior. I again remind you that this is not what you do when arguing has not worked. This is an immediate response to behavior before any argument. Let me use the child with the temper tantrum as an example. If a child is used to getting his own way if he throws a big enough temper tantrum, then decide to not let him have his own way. Just totally ignore his behavior until he realizes it is not going to work any more. Of course the tantrums will probably get worse first but that is all right if you can handle the noise. Just do not give him any indication at all that his tantrum is having any effect on you.

2. You could isolate the child for a specified period of time. Sometimes the fight will leave him if he has a little time alone. Being alone short-circuits any attempts he may have in mind to manipulate you or argue with you.

3. Rewarding a child for a positive behavior that is the opposite of the negative behavior you want to extinguish can be very effective. This is especially true if you can ignore the negative behavior. He will quickly learn that the positive behavior is more likely to get the positive attention he desires.

4. You could have his negative behavior cost him something that is valuable to him. Examples of this might be television time, video game time, having a friend over, or taking a part of his next allowance.

5. Allow natural consequences to occur. I am not suggesting that you let your child be burned to teach him not to put his hand on the hot stove. But, if he chooses to not put his dirty clothes

155

in the laundry room, then he can do without clean clothes until he does.

Whatever you do with spanking, remember that spanking is not an opportunity for you to vent your frustration or anger. Spanking is a very effective way to quickly change behavior. When it starts losing its effectiveness, then move on to another discipline technique.

CHAPTER NINETEEN

SUMMARY

Well, we have covered a lot of information in this book. Discipline is a difficult topic for most people. It is one of those topics that everyone seems to have an opinion about but so few understand. Discipline is one of the most influential things that shapes us into the people we become. One of the kindest things we can do for the children in our lives is to give them consistent, appropriate discipline. Discipline is like a pearl. It starts out seeming like a terrible irritant, but as you respond to that irritant appropriately, it becomes something very valuable. Discipline may not seem very pleasant at the time, but the end result is worth it all.

I would like to summarize this whole book with this:

20 WAYS TO RAISE A FAILURE

1. Start by giving your child everything he wants. That way he will grow up thinking the world owes him a living.

2. Always expect the worst from your child. That way you can act surprised when he does something right.

3. Remind your child that he is a miserable failure every time he makes a mistake.

4. Laugh at him and tell him how cute he is when he uses bad language. This will challenge him to be even more "cute."

5. Never do things together as a family. After all, you have your life to live and you really do not have time for him.

6.   Make lots of promises to him you do not keep. Tell him he needs to learn to be more flexible when he reminds you of your promise.

7.   Teach him that everything is relative and that there really is not a true right and wrong. That will help him avoid feeling guilty.

8.   Always do as much as you can for him. Clean his room, do his chores and other things he should normally do. That way he has more free time and does not have to worry about the burden of responsibility.

9.   Always solve as many of his problems, and make as many of his decisions for him, as possible. That way he does not have to get all stressed out at such an early age.

10.   Let the schools and churches have all the responsibility for his moral and spiritual training. After all, those topics are just too tough to deal with at home. By the way, do not expect him to go to church. Wait until he leaves home so he can decide for himself.

11.   Never let your child experience any discomfort. Always shield him from anything negative. After all, it is a cold, cruel world out there so he might as well be protected from it as long as possible.

12.   Let him read or have any kind of book or magazine he wants. After all, aren't all teenagers just naturally curious about that stuff?

13.   Let him watch all the smut he wants on television. Soap operas, free sex, and violence are simply part of this world today so he might as well watch it. You would not let a truck dump a load of garbage in your living room, but you let your television do it every day.

14. Expect your children to be perfect. Rule with an iron fist. Remember - You have to stay in total control. If they are not perfect then that means you are a failure too.

15. Have lots of arguments with your spouse in front of your child. That way he will not be so surprised when you get a divorce later.

16. Never let your child express his emotions. Remember that boys do not cry.

17. Rescue your child from the consequences of his behaviors. He needs you to protect him from himself. You do not want to risk him thinking you do not love him when you let him suffer the natural consequences of his behavior.

18. Always make sure that he has lots of money. Do not expect him to earn any of his own money. There is plenty of time for that later. After all, you had to work for your money when you were his age and you want him to have a better life.

19. Make sure your children believe that you are perfect. Of course to do that you will have to out-talk them and have a good excuse for anything that goes wrong. It is good for him to learn how to make good excuses for bad behavior anyway.

20. Always expect the worst. That way you can be sure your expectations will be met for many years to come.

Of course they are all facetious statements. You might be surprised, though, how many people would read them and think they were very wise statements. Oh well, enough said. I wish you well.

I wish you great patience and incredible wisdom as you go about fulfilling the greatest responsibility any person has ever had since the beginning of time: Raising a well-adjusted, responsible, moral, self-disciplined child.

SUGGESTED READINGS

1. Briggs, Dorothy, <u>Your Child's Self-Esteem</u>, Dolphin Books, N.Y. 1975

2. Price, Alvin H. and Parry, Jay A., <u>101 Ways to Boost Your Child's Self-Esteem</u>, American Baby Books, N.Y. 1982

3. Ackerman, Paul and Kappelman, Murray, <u>Signals: What Your Child Is Really Telling You</u>, Signet Books, N.Y. 1978

4. Gordon, Thomas, <u>Parent Effectiveness Training</u>, Wyden Books, N.Y. 1972

5. Hershey, Paul, Blanchard, Kenneth, <u>The Family Game</u>, Addison Wesley, N.Y. 1978

6. Stone and Church, <u>Childhood and Adolescence: A Psychology of The Growing Person</u>, Random House, N.Y. 1964

7. Fensterheim and Baer, <u>Don't Say Yes When You Want To Say No</u>, The David McKay Co., N.Y. 1970

8. Rubin, Theodore, <u>The Angry Book</u>, Collier MacMillan Co., N.Y. 1969

9. Simon and Olds, <u>Helping Your Child Learn Right From Wrong</u>, McGraw Hill 1977

10. Young, Leontine, <u>Wednesday's Children</u>, McGraw Hill, 1964

ABOUT THE AUTHOR

After 22 years of Counseling, Pastoring, Teaching, Coaching, and Mentoring literally thousands of people, Joel S. Leitch has come to realize that most people have very similar lists of frustrations and hopes for their children, their families, their friendships, and even themselves.

Joel is Internationally, Nationally, and State Licensed and Certified in 18 different specialties including Marriage, Family, & Adolescent issues, Acute & Post-Traumatic Stress Management and Debriefing, School Counseling and Crisis Response, Chemical Dependency & other addictions, and Criminal Justice. He has done other writing, including a book and training video on Suicide Prevention and Intervention. He is currently a Therapist in private practice in addition to teaching Introductory and Developmental Psychology as an Adjunct Faculty at a local college.

Printed in the United States
48573LVS00004B/1-102